Michael,

Best of luck in your new
position. I look forward to working
with you. I hope you enjoy my book
and find some useful ideas.

5-00

PASSING
THE
BUCKS

Norman A. Pappas

Passing the Bucks

Protecting Your Wealth from One Generation to the Next

Manufactured in the United States by:
  BookCrafters
  613 E. Industrial Drive
  P.O. Box 370
  Chelsea, Michigan 48118-0370

08 07 06 05 04 03 02 01 00 99   10 9 8 7 6 5 4 3 2 1

ISBN 0-9674518-0-9

Publisher's Cataloging-in-Publication
(Provided by Quality Books, Inc.)

Pappas, Norman A.
    Passing the bucks : protecting your wealth from one generation to the next / Norman A. Pappas. -- 1st ed.
      p. cm.
      Includes bibliographical references and index.
      ISBN: 0-9674518-0-9

    1. Estate planning--United States--Popular works. 2. Family-owned business enterprises--United States--Succession. 3. Inheritance and succession--United States--Popular works.
    I. Title.

KF750.Z9P37 1999   346.73'05
                        QBI99-1291

Designed by Catherine Biondi

Author's Note

Business succession planning, estate planning, and taxation are complex subjects, and the tax laws upon which this book is based may change. The information contained herein is not intended as specific tax or legal advice. Please consult your tax and/or legal advisors regarding your individual situation.

Table of Contents

Acknowledgement

I would like to thank a number of people for helping me to make this book a reality:

- **Jon Katz,** for helping me to present complicated technical material in common-sense language and a conversational style;

- **Catherine Biondi** and **Donna Coffey**, for their help in editing the book;

- My coworkers (**Neal Robin**, **Steve Gretchko**, **Janenne Howell**, and all the members of The Enterprise Group), for helping with the many details of putting the book together;

- My parents, **Charles and Sydell Pappas**, for giving me a thirst for knowledge; and

- My wife **Susie** and my children **Leslie**, **Dan**, and **Amy**, for their steadfast support.

Introduction

> *"It takes a great deal of boldness and a great deal of caution to make a great fortune, and when you have got it, it requires ten times as much wit to keep it."*
>
> —Ralph Waldo Emerson

The one esteemed financial goal that each of us has is to be set for life…and to have our spouse, our children and even our children's children financially secure as well.

Achieving this goal involves accumulation, preservation, and distribution of assets. Most of us spend much of our lives in the first two phases—the pursuit of accumulation to obtain and maintain sustenance and security. Very few of us, however, plan for the *final* phase—the distribution of these hard-earned assets to our successors.

It is ironic and, indeed, tragic that so many business owners devote their working lives to accumulating wealth for their families only to surrender 55% of it to estate taxes, potentially losing their businesses in the process.

They have fumbled the ball on the goal line. And they have lost the game as a result.

Yes, the estate tax is onerous. But it's one more thing:

It's optional!

There are strategies—effective and legal—for reducing the tax and earmarking your estate for more noble pursuits, such as family foundations. Such strategies don't jeopardize, but rather *enhance* your heirs' security, while at the same time increasing the legacy of your own life.

Just as it has been your life's goal to accumulate and preserve wealth, so it is your responsibility to plan its distribution in the most efficient manner possible.

The right financial plan asks and answers many questions. What did your mother's or father's life stand for? What sense of purpose did they have? What sense of purpose do you have? How can your business be preserved for future generations—not just for the family, but for the many employees who have dedicated their lives to the organization?

There are solid, dependable strategies that can help you resolve these important issues. They are not secrets; they are not "loopholes." What is unfortunate—and so costly—is that most people spend their working lives putting out "brush fires"—dealing with day-to-day financial concerns—while ignoring the oncoming "forest fire" of estate taxes. These people can end up losing 55% of their assets!

My purpose in writing this book is to make sure you don't become one of these people. I will help you to recognize potential problems and identify effective solutions—which, fortunately, are easy to learn and to implement.

I believe we should continue to improve ourselves by acquiring knowledge throughout our lives. Most of us have spent many years acquiring a formal education. Sometimes, however, the most useful information can be obtained in other ways. This book isn't a classic academic text, but it can help you to acquire some very important knowledge: how to preserve and pass on the fruits of your life's work to your heirs.

Passing the Bucks is intended primarily for business owners and people with taxable estates, but the principles and strategies presented in this book have applicability to almost everyone. Estate planning, apart from business succession, is critical to ensure that what you have worked so long and so hard to own—no matter how much or how little—will go where you intend.

I have structured the book like a series of one-on-one consultations, very much like I would conduct if you were here in my office. I've tried to make it easy to read, and have used non-technical language that's meant for *you*, not a financial advisor.

All of the costs, percentages, and assumptions I have used in this book are accurate as of the date of publication, but for updated information, I invite you to visit The Enterprise Group web site (www.theenterprisegroup.com). I promise you'll find it as easily digestible as the information you're about to read.

Once you learn the basics of business succession and estate planning, you'll find that a little knowledge is *not* a dangerous thing, but rather something crucial to preserving your business, your estate, and your legacy. So, let's get started *Passing the Bucks*!

Part One:

BUSINESS SUCCESSION PLANNING

1

The Business Succession Plan: What, Why, and When

Dear Business Owner and/or Heirs:

On behalf of the United States Government, thank you for leaving us your business. We certainly appreciate your not making any better plans to distribute the wealth you worked so many decades to accumulate. We're very much in your debt. Or is it the other way around?

Sincerely,
The Internal Revenue Service

You'll never get a letter like this one. You won't need to. Without a proper continuity plan that provides for the future of your business, your company may not *have* a future. As for the friendly folks at the IRS, they aren't really so cordial, nor their letters so witty.

Just what is a business succession plan?

Consider it a "business will." Just as your *personal* will determines what will become of your personal assets, a *business succession plan* determines what will become of your company.

And perhaps I wouldn't be far out of line to suggest that—given the years of devotion and dedication you've put into it—your business might very well be considered another "loved one" that must be provided for.

A complete plan consists of two parts: a **business succession plan**, which is a *long-term* strategy for the business when the owner retires, and a **strategic contingency plan**, which is a *short-term* strategy that becomes operational upon the unexpected loss of the owner through disability or death.

A good succession plan serves as a road map, effectively steering the company through the potentially hazardous twists and turns of transition from one owner (or group of owners) to the next.

That's fine for someone else. But I've already got a plan, right here in my head.

So does Bob. Bob is the owner and founder of a manufacturing company. His attorney recently approached him about planning for the company's future.

"I've got it all worked out," said Bob. "My son, David, will come into the firm when he finishes college. He'll take over when I retire. If something happens to me before that, Jim, my sales manager, can run the place until David's ready. Boom—there's my plan."

At least Bob has given some thought to the future of the business he has built. But his "plan" presents more problems than it solves:

- Has Bob discussed his plan with David and Jim?
- Do *their* plans for the future agree with his?
- Will Jim be willing to step aside when David says he's ready to take over?
- What training and experience is David receiving to prepare him to run the business?
- Will Bob eventually sell the business to David?
- If so, where will be money for the purchase come from?

It sounds complicated. I don't like complicated.

Business succession planning is certainly not as simple as it initially seems. Most business owners don't realize the range of issues involved, and the problems that can arise when a bad plan—or no plan—is in place. Even when an owner does recognize the critical need for planning, the complexity of the process and the difficult decisions that will need to be made often cause the owner to postpone taking action.

The costs of failing to plan are high:

Over 70% of family businesses fail to survive

into the second generation.

Over 85% fail before the third generation.

Why? Remember, I don't like complicated.

There are a number of unseen pitfalls that defeat the best intentions of owners, families, and managers. Let's take them one at a time.

Personal Issues

Succession planning can be emotionally distressing. In a closely held or family business, the owner (or owners) is often the person who has labored to build it from the ground up. After devoting a professional lifetime to the company, the thought of "letting go" can be very difficult.

When the owner does leave, not only is the captain gone, but perhaps the ship's directional "heading" may be called into question as well. If the ownership/management transition is not properly planned, infighting can occur as the crew—partners, managers and so on—jockeys for position and squabbles over the direction the organization will take.

Additional complexities arise when the company is a family-owned business. "Family" and "business" become intertwined, and it is often difficult to separate personal feelings from pragmatic business decisions. Parents and children may have differing expectations. Children may experience conflict between the desire to please their parents by "following in their footsteps," and the desire to find their own identity, inside or outside the company. Parents, meanwhile, endure conflicts of their own. They are torn between a sincere desire to allow their children the freedom to succeed and their fear of giving up control.

Avoiding these issues won't make them go away. Indeed, silence usually makes them worse. "I don't feel like discussing it today" does not prevent children, managers, and employees from forming their own ideas, opinions, and desires regarding the future of the company. When these issues are not addressed, they become expectations, then anxieties, and finally resentments.

In short, you end up sitting on a time bomb. If not defused with a proper plan, this bomb will explode, and the shrapnel will harm everyone around it.

Keyperson Issues

When a key individual (or individuals) has been the driving force behind the success of the business, and in effect *"is"* the business, the loss of this person can create a variety of operational problems. If the owner is a main source of revenue for the firm (based on client relationships or through services provided), income and cash flow may suffer after the departure. The owner may also have a key role in maintaining relationships with suppliers, banks, and other lenders. His or her loss could jeopardize these relationships and, accordingly, the organization's lines of credit.

Tax Issues

Tax issues can disrupt— if not totally sabotage—the transition of a business from one generation to the next. Consider the following statistics:

Tax Statistics	
Federal income tax costs	Typically 30-40%
State income tax costs	Typically 5% (varies by state)
Capital gains tax costs	18-40% (depending on duration held)
Estate tax costs	As high as 55%

Add on (or, more precisely, take away) the alternative minimum tax, generation skipping transfer taxes, and other taxes, and you begin to get the picture. It's certainly not a pretty one.

Neglecting to pay careful attention to tax issues can be financially disastrous. If you don't construct a plan to reduce or avoid transfer taxes, the business succession process may end up costing far more than it has to. Even worse, if you don't develop a strategy to pay personal estate taxes, your heirs may be forced to liquidate business holdings to meet the tax liability.

These tax issues should be examined by qualified specialists, who can create a cost-effective plan to minimize or even eliminate—*yes, eliminate*—taxes on the transfer.

Legal Issues

Even if you have a business succession plan in place, the succession process can fall apart if you haven't included appropriate legal instruments to implement and enforce the strategies that you and your successors agree on. Buy/sell agreements and stock voting agreements, for example, can establish a value for the business and stipulate the terms and conditions under which the transfer will take place. These documents can clearly specify definitions, values, and procedures which otherwise might generate conflict and resentment.

Your personal legal documents, such as wills and trusts, should be coordinated with the business succession plan to protect both your estate *and* the business from excess taxation, potential creditors, and probate exposure. Such planning will also ensure that your personal and business objectives are met.

Financial Issues

The best succession plan in the world cannot work if there is no money to carry it out. Consider funding stock redemption or cross-purchase agreements, and providing important benefits (such as retirement income for yourself, or executive benefits to retain key employees). Finally, you should have (and leave) enough liquidity for your heirs to pay your estate taxes without being forced to sell business holdings.

By establishing a succession plan, you will succeed in avoiding these and other pitfalls. Such a preemptive strike will then enable you to:

- determine your wishes for the future disposition of the business;
- decide on a successor (or successors);
- develop a plan to prepare your successor(s) for future responsibilities;
- anticipate and address any family or employee issues that may be generated by the succession plan;
- set aside any assets that may be required to enact the succession; and
- coordinate your personal and business finances to provide sufficient retirement income, fund any estate tax liability, etc.

The planning discussed so far can be a complex process, involving difficult decisions on issues both professional and personal. But the rewards are
worth it: a solid foundation for the survival and ongoing success of your
business; security and peace of mind for owners, managers and employees;
and, often, significant tax and financial advantages for both the owner and
the business.

***Okay, so I need a plan. But hey, I feel great, and my kids are still in
school. When should I start…really?***

It's never too late…and it's never too early. Bob, our manufacturing plant
owner, had similar feelings. When his attorney advised him to develop a
business succession plan as soon as possible, Bob commented, "I understand
that it's important to have a plan. I also see that there's a lot more to developing one than I thought. But I don't need to worry about it now. I plan on
staying around for a long time—and I mean that in a business sense and in
general. Besides," Bob went on, "there's a lot that may change in the years to
come. I don't see the point in planning for succession until I'm ready to think
about retirement."

Bob's right on one point. A lot *may* change over time. But that doesn't
mean that succession planning should be postponed. In fact, quite the oppo-
site is true. Time brings changes, and many of them will be unexpected.
Remember, your succession plan consists of two parts. And it's the second
part—the *strategic contingency plan*—that will provide for the unexpected.

Understand that succession planning is not a "death issue." It can—and
should be—a *living* issue. And if you live long enough to put the long-term
provisions to work, they may very well work for you for decades.

Succession planning should start from the time you have a viable business to pass on someday—no matter how far in the future that "someday" is.
However, the form that planning takes can—and should—change throughout
the lives of both the business and the owner. Chances are, your company will
pass through the following stages over the years:

- **Early stages**. Young business owners with newly established
  companies will not have the same concerns as owners considering
  retirement. In the first years of a business' life, the most vital issue
  is the growth and expansion of the company. Planning priorities

may include securing sources of financing for growth, establishing lines of credit, and covering business debt.

- **Middle stages.** In subsequent years, when businesses are running smoothly, owners' objectives will most likely change. Focus may no longer be on aggressive growth, but instead on such issues as ensuring steady expansion, developing future programs, and refining existing processes. At this stage, the issue of succession may arise, either directly or indirectly. While business owners may not be ready to consider retirement, they may become more concerned with key employees and managers, and the roles they play. If the owners have children, they may consider bringing them into the business at this stage, and mapping their future roles within the company.

- **Later stages.** As owners draw nearer to retirement, their business priorities will probably change again. They may now be more concerned about their personal financial futures, and will be less likely to take risks or make drastic business changes. They may want to begin phasing themselves out of the company, but may be afraid of letting go, or may be concerned about how they will handle the transition. Financial security and estate planning now become of real and present importance.

As you can see, business succession planning is not a "quick fix" that can be implemented on short notice. Succession planning is a *process*. It takes time to make decisions about succession, to obtain the agreement and commitment of all players, and to put the mechanisms of succession in place.

A plan should be considered and established early on, and then reviewed and revised regularly. Only in this way can you, the business owner with so much invested and so much to lose, keep up with the changing needs of both your business and the people involved.

Chapter Summary

- A *business succession plan* is a "business will" that lays out the future disposition of your business.

- An effective "business will" consists of two parts: a *business succession plan*, which spells out the long-term strategy for when the owner retires, and a *strategic contingency plan*, which is a short-term strategy to help the business through the inevitable crisis that occurs in the event of the unexpected loss of the owner.

- Over 70% of family businesses fail to survive into the second generation. Business succession planning, whether simple or complex, must be done to ensure the future success of the business and the financial security of the owner(s).

- Business succession planning proactively addresses the various personal, keyperson, tax, legal, and financial issues surrounding the transition of business ownership.

- Business owners should establish succession plans as soon as they have viable companies they wish to pass on someday.

- Succession planning is a process, not an event. Once established, a business succession plan should be reviewed and revised regularly to reflect the changing needs of both the owner and the company.

2

Succession Planning Basics

*"If you do not know where you are going, every
road will get you nowhere."*

—Henry Kissinger

The what, why, and when make good sense. Now...how?

I'm glad I've got you thinking. Planning is important, and it shouldn't be put off. Planning needn't be terribly complicated *if* you have a team of competent, qualified, and experienced advisors working with and for you.

But where do you begin?

Unfortunately, you can't open the *Yellow Pages* and turn to a category like "Succession, Business" or "Taxes, Minimizing" or "Son-in-Law, Putting Up With."

**So, how does a business owner go about finding help? How is a
plan developed and put into place?**

Your existing business advisors can provide a good starting point. Attorneys, CPAs, and bank officers are qualified sources of information. Depending on their levels of expertise, they may even be able to provide you with some of the assistance you need.

However, not all advisors have extensive experience in business and estate planning. Succession planning is a specialized task, and most advisors don't deal with the issue on a day-to-day basis. If this is the case, they may be able to recommend someone who can work with you *and* your existing advisors to develop a more creative and specific plan.

If you don't have advisors with whom you work closely, you can check other sources for information and referrals. Friends or colleagues may be able to recommend individuals they've worked with. Associations, trade groups, chambers of commerce, or the business department of a local college or university may also be able to assist you.

Whomever you choose to work with, keep this in mind: business planning is a complex process. And, like a custom-made suit, your plan must be tailored to your own personal needs. To develop the best plan, it is important that you consult with competent and trusted advisors. Your team should include at least one advisor who:

- specializes in business succession planning;
- has had significant experience in succession planning (specifically in family business planning, if your business is family-owned);
- is sensitive to the emotional issues involved in succession planning, and can work with the people involved to resolve these issues; and
- has a successful track record of helping other companies through the planning and transition process.

Unless you have one outstanding individual who can single-handedly do all your planning for you, it is best to work with a team of people. While one person may act as the catalyst for developing and implementing a plan, individuals with different areas of expertise help to balance the plan and make sure all your bases are covered.

The Planning Process

The number of issues involved in business succession planning can make the process itself seem overwhelming. But once you have selected your advisors, establishing your plan is more or less a matter of some very basic steps.

Note: you may wish to facilitate or coordinate action between your advisors, or you can select your most trusted advisor to lead the team.

In general, the planning process can be broken down into these basic concepts:

Planning Process	
Concept:	**Description:**
Analyze	Consider your (family) objectives
Design	Develop potential solutions
Obtain Feedback	Review the plan based on input from others
Revise	Make necessary changes
Implement	The most important step!

Here's how to go about getting the job done.

Analyze: Conduct Interviews to Determine the Issues and Circumstances Involved

Remember, a succession plan is a "business will" designed to carry out your wishes. You should consider certain questions such as who you want to take over your business, how much retirement income you will need, and so on. At this stage, you should conduct in-depth interviews with key individuals to get a broad perspective on the circumstances that should be considered in crafting an effective business succession plan.

In addition, meeting with your advisor (or advisors) can help you refine your objectives and address important issues about the status of the company. Your advisor can provide additional expertise, help ask the right questions, indicate potential pitfalls, and offer appropriate solutions.

Design: Create Your Business Succession Plan

Every business, every family, every individual is unique. Although there are a number of strategies and methods that are generally used in business succession planning, there is no such thing as a "boilerplate" solution. Like that custom-made suit I spoke of earlier, your advisor—your business "tailor"—should work closely with you to address your unique needs and concerns, and determine the strategy or combination of strategies that best meets those needs.

Based on your situation, your advisor should help you develop a plan that will:

- meet your objectives;
- minimize or eliminate taxes involved in the transition (income, estate, capital gains, etc.);
- allocate financial resources to fund the transition, if necessary; and
- utilize the proper tools to achieve these goals.

Gather Feedback: Review the Plan

Once the plan is laid out, the people involved—owner, family members, managers, etc.—should review the plan. As appropriate, incorporate their comments and recommendations into the final plan design.

Revise: Finalize the Plan

While it is not necessary for all of the key individuals to be consulted during the analysis phase, it is *vital* that they review and approve the final plan. Participants must be apprised of and acknowledge the issues and problems involved in the transition process, and agree that the plan provides a solution to these problems that satisfies the needs and expectations of everyone involved.

Implement: Put Your Plan in Place

Finalizing the plan is really the beginning of an ongoing process. Short-term objectives (such as drafting legal documents or establishing funding vehicles) must be carried out. Long-term goals (such as the development and training of the eventual successor) must be initiated. Over time, the plan should be re-examined and updated to conform to any changes in the company or in the objectives of those involved.

Just how long will it take to do all of this…and how much of **my time will my advisors need?**

Your team will do most of the work independently and, of course, the total time you spend is fully dependent on your specific circumstances. In general, the drafting process will proceed over a period of several months.

The actual time that you personally devote to this process may not be more than just a few hours…which isn't much of an investment to preserve a lifetime of work.

Fine. I'm okay with ongoing processes. But you make it sound **too** *simple. I mean, these advisors of mine had better have lots of questions for me, because there's a lot about my business that nobody but* **me** *knows.*

Agreed. Let's start with the strategic contingency plan. Remember, your "business will" is made up of two parts: a long-term *business succession plan*, and a short-term *strategic contingency plan*. The strategic contingency plan is designed to guide the business through a crisis period in the event of the sudden and unexpected loss of an owner due to circumstances such as death or disability.

No one expects such events to occur, but unfortunately, they sometimes do. The 1996 plane crash in Bosnia, in which U.S. Commerce Secretary Ron Brown and a number of prominent American businessmen and women were killed, is one tragic example.

The emotional strain and administrative vacuum created by such a loss can be devastating. Your strategic contingency plan will provide emergency guidance and direction for your family and your company. It is a stopgap measure that will ensure that your business continues to function.

As a business owner, you are in control of your company. Now, you need to take control of your life. The job can be a smooth one, but it *is* a job. As individuals who have established net worth get older, it becomes incumbent upon them to determine, once they're financially secure, how they will take care of those who depend on them.

Imagine that it is the day after your unexpected death or disability. The following questions should be considered in developing your plan.

I. Business Operations

    A. Will the company be "open for business"? Who has keys to the building or office? Who has access to your personal office, files, and information?

    B. Which people know the location of, and have access to, important business papers such as articles of incorporation, stock certificates, tax returns, etc.?

C. Who will temporarily operate the business? Does this person know that he or she will be in charge? Will he or she accept the responsibility?

D. How will business decisions be made? Which people will have the authority to make them?

E. What will the lines of authority and responsibility be?

F. Who should be contacted (clients, suppliers, bank officers, CPAs, attorneys)?

II. Financial Considerations

A. How will your loss affect the company cash flow?

B. Is there a line of credit that was secured by you? Will this need to be repaid? Where will the money come from?

C. Will your loss affect the company's terms of credit with banks, lenders, investors, or suppliers?

D. What should be done about payables, receivables, etc.? Will cash need to be conserved, at least temporarily? What changes need to be made to the financial aspects of the business? Who will make these decisions?

E. Will your existing clients and suppliers continue to work with your company? Do your clients and suppliers know other contacts within the company besides you? Are they comfortable with these other relationships?

III. Personal Issues

A. How will your loss affect your spouse and/or children?

B. Does anyone in your family know where to find important personal information (wills, trusts, insurance policies, etc.)?

C. Does anyone in your family have an inventory of your assets (bank accounts, investments, deeds, etc.)?

D. How will your family's financial situation be affected? Where will their income come from? Will they have enough money to maintain their standard of living? Are there business or personal debts for which they will become responsible?

E. Does your family know your wishes with regard to both personal and business matters? Will your family be involved in either taking over the business or disposing of it? Are they prepared for these responsibilities? Are they aware of advisors or other resources that can assist them if necessary?

IV. Longer-Term Considerations

A. Who should eventually take over ownership of the business on a permanent basis? Who should eventually run the business? Should the same person (or people) do both?

B. What kind of plan (if any) is in place to ensure that these transitions occur? Is the plan simply a verbal agreement, or has it been formalized (i.e., in the form of a buy/sell agreement)?

C. How will the plan be affected by your sudden loss? If the plan triggers a buyout, where will the money come from?

D. Will your key employees (and other employees) remain with the company through the crisis period? Will competitors attempt to hire them away? Are there any incentives, safeguards, or assurances in place to help retain these people?

Whoa, let me catch my breath!

Yes, I know it's a lot to think about. But if you spend a little time *now* to answer these questions and to plan, it will save enormous amounts of time later for your family.

Okay. Now...let's assume I'm around long enough to retire, so nobody has to look for my keys or call the clients. What are the long-term questions my advisors will ask?

There are essentially four options for the disposition of any business— what we might call "owner exit strategies." The company can be:

- liquidated;
- sold to an outside party;
- retained and transferred to family or key employees through a sales transaction; or
- retained and transferred to family or key employees through gifting.

The liquidation of a business or sale to an outside party present specific and unique sets of issues which will be covered in Chapter 6. The questions that follow will address the third and fourth options: transferring your business to family members and/or key employees by sale or gift.

Again, every business is different, and your situation will vary according to the type of business you own, whether you have a closely held or family business, and what your particular family and financial situations are. The questions below will provide a starting point for developing your succession plan.

I. Ownership Issues

A. Which family members will receive ownership of the business?

B. Are there non-family members who should also receive some ownership?

C. If you are transferring ownership to more than one person, what percentage of ownership should each person receive? Should there be any provision for future buyouts?

D. Should the transfer of ownership be made all at once, or gradually over a period of time?

E. How will the transfer be accomplished?
Gifting: should business assets be gifted to children or other recipients? Should the gift be made outright, or should a specialized vehicle such as a trust or family partnership be used? How can the gifts be made with minimal or no tax consequences?
Sale: should the business be sold to family members? What is a fair selling price? What should the terms of the sale be? Where will the money for the purchase come from?

F. Have you discussed your goals and plans with the other people involved (children, key managers, spouse)? Do they share your objectives?

II. Management Issues

A. Should the people who eventually *own* the business be the same ones who *run* the business?

B. What additional experience and/or training will your management successors need?

C. What is the best way for them to gain this knowledge?

D. What are your key business relationships (clients, suppliers, bankers, advisors)? Do they know your successors? Will they be as willing to work with your successors as they have been able to work with you? What steps need to be taken to strengthen these relationships?

III. Key Employee Issues

A. Are there key employees that you wish to retain? Non-family employees in a family business may think their future within the company is limited because family members will always take precedence.

B. What steps have you taken to ensure that these key employees will stay on?

IV. Personal Planning Issues

A. Once the business is sold or otherwise transferred, where will your retirement income come from?

B. How will the transfer of the business affect your personal estate planning?

C. Have you calculated your estate taxes? How will they be paid?

D. If you are transferring the business to your children or other heirs, you are leaving them with a significant asset. Are there other children who will not be involved in the business, but still need to be provided for?

Obviously, many of these questions have no simple answers. In order to make informed decisions, more information—about pros and cons, about possible options, and about potential consequences—must be obtained. In the next several chapters, I will examine some of these difficult decisions, and provide you with guidelines for analyzing your own situation.

Chapter Summary

▪ Your existing business advisors can be a good source of information and assistance in developing your business succession plan, either through their own expertise or by providing you with referrals to other qualified advisors.

▪ Succession planning requires experience and technical expertise. At least one of your advisors should specialize in business succession planning (and, specifically, in family business planning, if you have a family-owned business). He or she should have extensive experience and a good track record of assisting other companies through the planning and transition process.

▪ The planning process is one of discussion, analysis, feedback, and revision. There are five basic steps in the process:

- analyze: determine the circumstances and issues involved;
- design: create your business succession plan;
- gather feedback: review the plan;
- revise: finalize the plan; and
- implement: put your plan in place.

▪ When creating a strategic contingency plan, you should think about:

- business operations;
- financial considerations;
- Personal issues; and
- longer-term considerations.

▪ When creating a business succession plan, you should think about:

- ownership issues;
- management issues;
- key employee issues; and
- personal planning issues.

3

Who Gets the Business: Ownership Succession and Management Succession

"The best executive is the one who has the sense

enough to pick good men to do what he wants

done, and self-restraint enough to keep from

meddling with them while they do it."

—Theodore Roosevelt

The most fundamental—and perhaps the most difficult—succession planning decision that a business owner must make is, *Who will be my successor?*

Choosing a successor can be a complex, difficult, and emotionally charged decision. If you are like most business owners, your company represents something very important and highly personal to you: years of hard work and sacrifice. It is the embodiment of your success, the symbol of your achievement.

And in addition to this sense of personal accomplishment, your company represents your financial success, the "golden goose" that has allowed you to provide for your family, your employees, and yourself.

Because your business is so important—and so personal—to you, it may be difficult to think about the company continuing without you. The thought of someone else "taking over" may generate a lot of mixed feelings.

Take the example of Simon, the 57-year-old owner of a prosperous distribution company. Simon has a 32-year-old son, Alan, and a 30-year-old daughter, Rachel, who both work in the business.

Simon is starting to think about retirement. He founded his company nearly 35 years ago, and has built it into a successful firm. But Simon is starting to get burned out by the travel and long hours, and he would like to start working less, to the point of eventually removing himself from the business entirely. Simon would like his children to take over the company, but he finds himself hesitating to make definite plans for this to happen.

While retirement appeals to Simon, he has some concerns. He worries about how the business will do without him. Although he respects his son and daughter, he wonders if they are really "ready" to run things on their own. And while he is proud to be able to leave a financially successful company to his children, he wonders if they will fully appreciate his legacy. Do they understand his hard work and sacrifice, and truly appreciate the opportunity he is providing for them?

Simon's concerns are understandable, and quite common. Many business owners are torn between the desire to leave something of value for their children—to provide them with the opportunity to achieve their own success—and concern for the future of the business they have built.

The same feelings apply in situations where non-family members, such as key managers, are slated to take over the company. You want the business to continue and succeed, but you may worry that no one else can run it like you can. This is understandable: you have a genuine concern for the company that you have built. But your concern may also mask more personal fears about what your own role will be once you step aside. You may fear losing your purpose, self-worth, or identity.

Perhaps the most important step in succession planning occurs when you come to a psychological resolution and are *ready* to let go. More than one business has failed because the owner retired and then came back to "straighten things out," or because they delegated authority to successors and then undermined it when it conflicted with their own ideas. Your successors need to be given the opportunity to soar on their own, to try—and occasionally fail—in order to learn, and to gain the confidence and experience they need to succeed.

Instead of thinking about your departure from the company as a loss—a loss of the business, a loss of income, and especially a loss of self-esteem or purpose—imagine it as an opportunity, a chance to take the time to explore other interests.

If you desire a longer transition, it is possible to maintain a role in the company on a part-time or consulting basis, as long as you respect the new lines of responsibility and authority that you have created.

Most importantly, the act of passing a business on to the next generation is an opportunity to leave something of value that will endure beyond your own lifetime. Passing on the business not only leaves a valuable asset that can provide security and opportunity for future generations, it also provides a legacy of your own personal values. The business is the symbol of your hard work, persistence, sacrifice, and dedication. In taking over the business, your successors inherit not only the business itself, but also the philosophy and values that are its foundation—values that will impact and guide them for the rest of their lives.

Well, I can identify with Simon. I'm lucky; I've got a couple of good kids who will one day join the firm, and some top employees, too. So how do I decide who takes over the business?

When considering who will be your successor, the choice may appear to be obvious. Your initial reaction may be "my son/daughter/children" (if the company is a family business) or "my top sales executive/financial officer/ plant manager" (if the company is a closely held business). However, the decision is not necessarily as cut-and-dried as it seems.

The question of who will take over the business raises two separate but equally important issues:

- **Who will *operate* the business?** As any business owner knows, running a business is a complicated task that requires a great deal of knowledge, experience, energy, organization, and dedication. Which person is best suited to take on this task? Which person has the management skills, financial acumen, and market savvy to lead the company forward to continued success?

- **Who will *own* the business?** Your company represents a significant economic asset. The inherent value of the company, combined with its potential to provide additional income (through revenues, dividends, rents, etc.), makes it a valuable legacy to pass on. Which person should receive the economic benefits of ownership?

In the simplest situation, your successor will be someone capable of both owning and operating the business. Perhaps you have a son working in the company who is being trained to take over the business after you. Or, perhaps you have arranged to sell the business to your vice-president, a loyal long-service employee. You will be able to provide a valuable asset to your successor, receive a fair value for your business, and be secure in the knowledge that you are leaving your business in competent hands.

However, most situations are not so simple. Let's return to Simon, our 57-year-old distribution company owner who is starting to think about retirement. As he considers his succession plan, Simon is faced with several confusing and apparently conflicting issues:

- Simon wants his son Alan and his daughter Rachel, both of whom have worked in the company for several years, to inherit the business. Rachel, who has an MBA in finance and is currently the head of the accounting department, has stronger overall business skills than Alan does. However, Alan is an outstanding sales executive who, as regional manager of the eastern sales division, has been responsible for the company's large market share increase over the last five years. Alan and Rachel have very different personalities, and Simon doesn't feel that they would be able to share the leadership between them. How does he decide which child will be his successor?

- Simon's business, which is worth about $6 million, makes up the majority of his personal net worth and is his main source of income. If anything were to happen to him, his wife, Elizabeth, would have little or no financial support. Should he leave the business to her in order to provide her with needed income?

- There are three employees—a vice president, a marketing director, and a regional sales manager—who have been with the company for a long time. These individuals have played an important role in the growth and success of the business. Simon would like to reward these employees for their loyalty and hard work. How can he provide for them as well?

Simon's concerns raise a number of specific questions about both his succession plan and his personal planning.

Who Should Run the Business?

Simon seems to think that Rachel would be the better choice to take over the leadership of the company. However, he also recognizes Alan's contributions, and feels a sense of responsibility to him. At this point, Simon feels that it would be impossible to choose between them.

Simon needs to sort through several issues—and his own emotions—to determine what is really involved in this decision. The real question is *Who is best suited to fill the position Simon is leaving?* This decision is not about who inherits the business, or even about what kind of inheritance each child will receive. And it is certainly not about "picking a favorite" among the children.

Only if Simon is able to put family and emotional considerations aside, understanding that they are truly separate issues, can he recognize that he is making an administrative decision about who is the best person for the job. After all, if Simon were considering two *employees* (as opposed to offspring) for a promotion, on what basis would he make his decision? Considering which of his children will run the business after he retires is really no different. If Simon were to make a decision on any other grounds, he could put the business at risk. Selecting the wrong person for the wrong reasons could impair the future growth and security of the company. If the business were lost through poor management, what benefit would it be to either of Simon's children?

There are a number of factors that can help Simon make a reasonable, sound decision.

First, does he have any idea what Alan and Rachel want? If only one of them is interested in taking over full operation of the business, then there is no conflict to be resolved, and Simon's anxiety over appearing to favor one child over the other is groundless.

Second, unless Simon is going to retire tomorrow, the decision does not have to be made right away. Simon can begin to give both Rachel and Alan additional responsibilities, and see how they handle their new roles. This should certainly not be seen as a "contest" between the two children. But it is a means to evaluate their various talents, and to see who is most suited for the leadership role.

Finally, Simon needs to remember that choosing one of his children as his successor does not mean that the other child has no future in the company. Either Rachel or Alan could fill important roles within the company—as corporate officers, regional or department managers, or heads of special projects. Simon's business is large enough and prosperous enough to allow both Alan and Rachel space to create their own roles and successes within it. Management succession will be discussed in greater detail in the following chapter.

Who Will Inherit the Business?

Because Rachel and Alan will have a great deal of responsibility for the operation of the business, Simon feels it would only be fair for them to enjoy ownership as well. But he is also concerned about his own retirement, and about his wife's financial security.

One possible solution would be for Simon to retain ownership of the business stock until his death, and then pass it to his wife Elizabeth, who would then pass it to their children. However, he and Elizabeth will probably live for 20 to 30 more years. This seems like a long time to make his children wait to inherit the business that they will be operating in only a few years.

There are other drawbacks: first, if Simon dies and Elizabeth inherits the business stock, then Alan and Rachel will, in effect, be working for their mother, which may be an awkward and undesirable situation. In addition, all of Elizabeth's income will come from company stock, and will therefore be dependent on the success of the business. If the business hits a slump, Elizabeth's financial security could be threatened.

Leaving the stock to Rachel and Alan—either during Simon's lifetime (by gifting or selling the stock) or at his death (through his will)—is also problematic. If Elizabeth survives Simon, she will have little or no income after Simon's death. And if the stock is gifted to the children during his lifetime, both he and Elizabeth may find their income compromised.

Selling the stock to the children could provide a solution, giving Simon and Elizabeth liquid assets in exchange for the stock; however, it is doubtful that Rachel and Alan have the $6 million required to carry out the purchase.

In some ways, determining the ownership of the business—who gets the business stock, as well as when and how they receive it—is more difficult than determining a successor. A host of financial concerns arise, from retirement income and financial security for you and your spouse, to economic security for your successors, to the fiscal strength of the company itself. The business may start to seem like the proverbial goose that lays the golden eggs—you can't divide it up without destroying it.

Ownership of the company's stock also raises issues of control. Who will the shareholders be? How much influence will they have in making important business decisions? What if you want to leave some of your stock to children working for the company, and some to other children not in the business? Will those children who are not involved in the business have an equal say in the decision-making process?

Fortunately, there are creative and effective strategies that will enable you to address all of these situations. The various methods for transferring ownership will be discussed later in this book.

How Do I Reward Other Employees?

In thinking about your succession plan, you may realize that you have employees who, for various reasons, aren't candidates to be your successor, but you may still wish to provide for them in your "business will."

For example, maybe you plan to sell your business to your sales manager, but your office manager, bookkeeper, and warehouse supervisor have provided valuable service over the years and you'd like to reward them for their loyalty and support.

Rewarding key employees becomes even more important in a family-owned business. Long-service, loyal employees—whose ideas about their future with your company may have included a significant managerial or even an ownership role—may get discouraged when they realize that your son or daughter will be the one to reap the biggest future rewards. Non-family employees working for a family business may feel that their prospects are limited and that their contributions will always be secondary to those of your relatives.

There are a number of incentives that can be used to retain and reward key employees, and to encourage them to remain with the company and continue to provide their valuable services. These incentives will be addressed in later chapters.

Choosing your successors—for both ownership and management—can be a difficult and confusing task, but it isn't an impossible one. Don't be tempted to avoid the difficult issues. Thinking about and resolving these questions now will give you the peace of mind that comes with knowing that the future of your business, as well as your own financial security, are provided for in a way that reflects *your* preferences.

Chapter Summary

- The most fundamental—and perhaps the most difficult—succession planning decision you must make is who your successor will be.

- The most important step in succession planning is to decide that you are ready to let go and let others start to take over. Too many businesses have been ruined by owners who "retired" but couldn't keep their hands off the business.

- Deciding who will take over your business really addresses two questions: (1) who will *operate* the business, and (2) who will *own* the business? The answers may or may not point to the same person.

- Addressing the issue of a successor will most likely raise some difficult questions, such as:

  - How do I choose just one person to succeed me? In particular, how do I decide among my children in a family business?

  - Once I leave the business, how do I provide financial security for my spouse and me?

  - How do I reward and retain key employees?

- Don't despair if succession decisions seem difficult or impossible. Many business owners are tempted to avoid the hard questions rather than address uncomfortable topics. There *are* answers, and resolving these issues now will provide you with security and peace of mind.

4

Management Succession: Choosing and Training Future Leaders

"Nearly all men can stand adversity, but if you want to test a man's character, give him power."

—Abraham Lincoln

You seem to have knocked the wind out of me again—thanks. But I see that ownership and management succession can be, as you said, separate but equally important. So where do I start picking a team to run the place?

You may feel overwhelmed at the number of complex issues that are raised in considering a successor. Remember, you *don't* need to make these decisions on your own. Very few business owners are fortunate enough to have simple, unambiguous plans for management and ownership succession. For most people, the decisions are not so simple. In these situations, a number of strategies can help you come up with the best solutions.

Formulate Vision and Mission Statements

Taking the time to create vision and mission statements will:

- define the goals and values of your business;
- clarify your company's focus and purpose;
- identify the personal values, principles, and ideals that are the foundation of your business philosophy; and
- give you an opportunity to map out a business strategy for the future.

Focusing on these issues can you help you clarify the personality and business traits you're looking for in a successor, and help you to identify an individual who will be able and willing to uphold your values and meet the strategic goals of the business.

Test the Waters

When you decide to choose a successor, it is not necessary to simply "pick" someone immediately. Begin by identifying potential candidates, and by assisting these individuals in career development by gradually giving each person additional responsibility. Their strengths and weaknesses may become apparent in how they handle their new roles, potentially narrowing the field. In time, the best candidate may become apparent.

Attempt a Consensus

If you own a family business, and if your family relationships are strong and open enough, you may be able to discuss the succession issue with your relatives to reach a mutual agreement.

Be aware that such a discussion may bring strong emotions, conflicts, resentments, and rivalries to the surface. If you are not comfortable talking about and sorting through potentially troublesome family issues, this may not be the best method for you. However, the great advantage of this method is that, since the decision is a *consensus,* all family members agree on and support the decision.

Seek Outside Opinions

Many companies have a board of directors, composed of respected peers and advisors who are not directly involved in the business. These people can provide a fresh perspective, removed from internal pressures and conflicts, which can be invaluable in making a decision.

Enlist the Help of a Professional Advisor

Experienced succession planning advisors can provide objective advice and help you sort through the issues to help determine goals and objectives.

They can also provide you with the proper techniques and strategies to best meet those goals.

So now that I've settled on the people who'll carry on the company, now what do I do? They still don't know a fraction of what it's taken me a lifetime to learn.

Many people think that training a successor begins only after that person has been specifically chosen. This is not necessarily true. On the most basic level, every employee starts learning about your business from the first day they start working for the company. But even "job-specific" training can—and should—start long before employees' future roles are set in stone.

This does *not* mean, however, that the day your son starts working in your business, you should start him on the path that leads to the CEO's office. Establishing roles and expectations too early can lead to frustration and resentment. Your son may feel "forced" into a position he is not sure he wants; you may have second thoughts as to whether he is the best person for the job. Fear of disappointing someone or of hurting someone's feelings can make it difficult to back out of a hasty decision, leading to anger, embarrassment, and frustration later if things don't work out.

Early training means that each person's career should develop along a sensible path. All of your employees should expand their skills, take on additional duties, and learn other aspects of the business. This is especially true for successors and key managers, who have the greatest responsibility and authority. By mapping out career paths and *slowly* delegating additional responsibilities, you can determine how well each person performs, and what their talents and affinities are.

It is also important to find out whether successors and managers enjoy their new roles. Sometimes the "big chair" looks appealing from the outside, with its economic benefits, executive perks, and perceived freedom, but some people may not realize just how much responsibility and hard work are involved in running a business.

The wise business owner, like a chess master, takes stock of all his or her "pieces" and carefully considers where, when, and how to move them. You should have a strategy in mind, but be sure to keep it flexible. It's far easier to leave "Plan A" behind when you already have a "Plan B" ready.

As you start moving your key players along the paths you are considering for them, you may find weaknesses that you didn't know existed. This gives you the opportunity to provide additional training and experience to compensate for any shortcomings individuals may have, or to reconsider their candidacy altogether. On the other hand, you may also come across undiscovered strengths that can benefit your business now and in the future.

I'm a fly-by-the-seat-of-the-pants kind of person, but I sure don't want the person running my company to be the "daredevil" I was. What's the best training method?

The more your successor knows about all aspects of the business, the better he or she will be able to run the company someday. Exactly what type of training is best for your successor—how much should consist of "hands on" experience and how much should consist of formal education or other preparation—will vary depending on the type of business, and on the person. A number of approaches can be used, alone or in combination, depending on what is appropriate for your business.

The "Ground-up" Approach

Many business owners believe in the "ground-up" approach—that a future successor should learn about a business by actually working his or her way up the company's corporate ladder.

For example, in a manufacturing firm, the successor might start out working on the assembly line, then become a plant or warehouse manager, and eventually move into executive management.

This approach certainly provides a well-rounded corporate education. In a family business, this method has the added advantage of eliminating animosity from non-family employees who might resent any perceived "special privileges" granted to family members.

This approach, however, can also take time, which may be impractical for your situation. It is most useful if you have a young successor whom you can nurture and train over a long period. Learning all aspects of the business can instill an understanding of how the many parts of the business work together, as well as an appreciation of the hard work involved.

Mentoring

Another approach is to provide the successor with a mentor who can act as a role model and provide advice and guidance along his or her career path. The mentor could be someone within the company, or an outside person such as an executive working in a related industry.

If your business is family-owned, your successor's mentor should not be a relative—especially not a parent. In such a relationship, there is too much potential for emotions and anxieties to overlap with business decisions. It is highly recommended that, for as long as possible, children working in the business should not report directly to parents, siblings, or other relatives. Working with a non-family mentor allows your successor to learn and grow while focusing on the expectations of the job, instead of worrying about the expectations of a relative.

Outside Experience

Experience working for another company can give your successor a different, and therefore valuable, perspective. Businesses—and their owners—often get used to doing things "the way they've always been done." An outside perspective, whether from a similar or unrelated industry, can bring new insights, ideas, and processes that can revitalize your company and give it new life and direction.

Some amount of outside experience is particularly useful for family successors. Such experience can foster a sense of accomplishment that is not dependent on the artificially "friendly" structure of a family-owned business. Working outside the company can provide an opportunity for family members to prove that they are able to succeed on their own merit in the "real" world. In addition, people who have worked exclusively in family-owned companies may feel tempted to leave when things get rough, reasoning that any problems they are experiencing are brought about by family concerns rather than business-related issues. Working for another organization can show your children that the grass isn't necessarily greener elsewhere.

That's for sure. I especially like the part about "an appreciation of the hard work involved." Any other tips to avoid future conflicts?

- **Set *attainable* goals and *measurable* objectives, and establish accountability.** As potential successors take on new responsibilities, make sure they understand the objectives associated with their new positions. Don't simply tell someone that you want him or her to "increase sales." What exactly does that mean? Are you aiming to beat last year's sales percentages, increase current market share, or penetrate new markets? Instead of being vague, objectives should be measurable so that you can objectively evaluate an individual's performance.

  Discuss goals and objectives in detail with your employees and make sure they understand and agree to them. Then, make sure you hold each individual accountable. If sales did not increase as projected, why not?

  Objective setting and accountability are particularly important in a family business. By setting challenging but attainable objectives, your successor can achieve measurable successes. This demonstrates (to you, to your successor, and to non-family employees) that your successor's position in the company is based on merit, not on favoritism.

  In addition, by establishing accountability, you demonstrate that your successor will be held responsible for his or her actions. Participation in the family business is a privilege, not a right, and family members should not simply "expect" to have a job in the company.

- **Establish clear lines of responsibility and authority.** Job descriptions should be well defined. Make sure each person knows what his or her duties are, what their business objectives are, and to whom he or she is accountable. Knowing exactly who is responsible for what helps to clarify roles and to avoid stepping on toes. If at all possible, avoid conflict and resentment by not requiring family members to report directly to one another. Business and management conflicts can too easily become family squabbles.

- **Establish different career paths for different successors.** In training your successors, try to establish different career paths for each of them. If potential successors all follow the same "route," it may invite competition and comparisons as to who is doing a better job. In addition, succession candidates may feel limited by the progress of those who have taken the path ahead of them; they may feel they are unable to advance any further until someone gets out of the way. By establishing different paths—preferably ones that focus on your successors' strengths—you allow each potential successor to establish his or her own focus and identity free of rivalries and comparisons.

▪ **Allow potential successors to take on responsibilities without undue interference.** As a succession candidate's training progresses, you will most likely start handing off some of your own responsibilities to him or her. This can be a difficult transition for a business owner to make. However, it is important to give your future successors a chance to succeed on their own. Once you delegate, *hands off.* Don't fall into the trap of giving someone authority and then countermanding it, or of letting someone head up a project and then stepping in to show them how to do it. These practices are counterproductive, and will lead to resentment and ineffectiveness.

▪ **Set rules for participation in a family business.** In a family business, it is important to have guidelines for family members in terms of both participation in, and ownership of, the business. You may wish to address questions such as:

- Who is considered "family"? Does the term include only immediate descendants, or does it also include cousins, step-children, and in-laws?

- What skills and experience are needed to be able to work in the business?

- And, perhaps most importantly, how much participation is required for someone to be eligible to own equity in the business? Family members may view the company as a "money pie," and feel that they are entitled to a piece. This is especially true when the business makes up a large part of the parents' estate. Establishing a written policy lets everyone know what it takes to earn the privileges of participation and ownership.

- In addition, it's a good idea to establish salary guidelines, standards for performance reviews and promotions, and so on. This establishes a set of ground rules to let everyone know what is expected, and to ensure fair treatment of family and non-family members alike.

There are a lot of issues here, and many of them can be emotionally charged and dangerous if not handled well. Whatever the path chosen for successors from within the family, employees should look at "Junior" as the wave of the future who will provide for their security. The fact that he's here today in whatever capacity is a sign that the company—and their jobs—will be there tomorrow…and it's to everyone's benefit to help him succeed.

Preparing a successor to take over your business is a process: the gradual handing-over of additional duties and responsibilities. A well-planned transition will map out career paths, goals and objectives, and key points in the succession process. In an ideal succession plan, the transition should happen so smoothly that it's hardly noticeable.

Chapter Summary

- Various strategies can help you define the criteria for selecting a successor, including:
    - formulating company vision and mission statements;
    - determining potential successors' strengths and weaknesses;
    - reaching a consensus about succession among family members in a family-owned business;
    - seeking opinions from outside peers and advisors; and
    - enlisting the help of an experienced succession planning advisor.
- Training your successor should start even before a successor has been officially chosen.
- Early training can help compensate for successors' weaknesses, take advantage of their strengths, and provide you with the information you need to alter your succession plan if necessary.
- Training a potential successor may involve one or more of the following:
    - taking a "ground-up" approach to allow succession candidates to learn all aspects of the business, from entry-level through management;
    - pairing the person with a mentor to provide individualized training and guidance; and
    - requiring the individual to obtain work experience outside the business.
- Successor training and development should follow a well-defined path, and should:
    - set measurable performance objectives and establish accountability;
    - establish clear lines of authority and responsibility;
    - allow potential successors to take on responsibilities without undue interference;
    - establish varying career paths for different succession candidates; and
    - set ground rules for participation in a family business.

5

Group Benefits and "Golden Handcuffs": Attracting and Keeping Your Employees

"To attract the best talent, you must provide a stimulating and attractive work environment. Great employees won't work for a company just for the money."

—Rick Eigenbrod
American Business Author
and Consultant

When choosing and training your successor, remember that even though this person will play a vital role in the future of your company, he or she will not be working alone. Every successful business owner depends on one or more key employees who excel at their jobs, who keep things running smoothly and effectively, and who make significant contributions to the success of the company.

But as every business owner knows, such employees are hard to come by. A top priority in any succession plan should be attracting—and retaining—the very best people.

When a business owner retires or otherwise leaves, the company experiences a period of transition. Roles and responsibilities may change; new processes may be put into place. Until people settle into the new routine, there may be tension and uncertainty about the capabilities of the new management regime and, indeed, about the very future of the company.

Employees may also feel uncertain about their own futures. During the transition, the changes that have been mapped out in the succession plan are taking place. There may be promotions and a shifting of responsibilities as the company reorganizes to fill the gap left by the departing owner.

As the new order takes effect, employees may question both their current roles and their future opportunities. For example:

- A key employee who has been with the company for twenty years may resent the fact that someone with less seniority has been given a higher position in the company.

- An executive who enjoyed a good working relationship with the departing CEO may not be sure that he or she will get along with the new one.

- A manager may take a look at the new corporate structure, assume that the new roles will be in place for some time, and decide that future possibilities suddenly don't look as good as they did in the past.

- Non-family employees may fear that their prospects will always be limited in a family business.

All of this means that employees—particularly key employees who know their value—may be tempted to look elsewhere for what they consider better opportunities.

Retaining key employees is important not only during a transition period: it should be an ongoing concern for any business owner. Today's job market is increasingly competitive as corporations scramble to hire the best people. In a time of corporate downsizing, employees may have less company loyalty when they feel they have less job security. They may be more likely to change jobs more often, lured by competitors with a better offer. They may decide that it's best to look out for themselves if they are uncertain that the company will take care of them.

Unfortunately, you're right on all counts. So short of giving away the store, how do I hold on to my best people?

The best way to retain top-notch employees is to give them a good reason to stay. And in my experience, the best incentive is a compensation package that provides valuable benefits and is competitive with other businesses in your industry.

The two most obvious ways to enhance your employees' compensation package are to (1) increase salaries, and (2) to provide enhanced or additional group benefits. But these "obvious" answers may not be the best solutions.

Why not?

Salary increases, obviously, mean that more money will be flowing out of your company. And in addition to the actual salary increase amounts, there are increased payroll taxes to consider. The grossed-up figure makes pay raises an unattractive solution for many business owners. But even if your company can afford the higher overhead, there are other reasons why more money may not be the best answer.

A salary increase provides an *immediate* benefit. A raise is "money in the pocket" that employees can enjoy and appreciate *today*. But because the raise is a benefit that is received *now*, it's not necessarily an incentive for employees to stay with you in the future. If they were to receive a higher offer from another company, there would be nothing to keep them from accepting.

So, what is the best solution?

Instead of (or in addition to) a salary increase, consider offering "perks" that may be unique to your company, or that would be hard to find somewhere else. This may include company cars; use of the company's season tickets for sporting or theater events; or the opportunity to purchase goods or services produced by your company at a discount or at cost.

An even better alternative is to provide benefits where the payoff occurs at some point in the future. This gives employees an incentive to stay with you in order to reap that eventual reward. These types of benefits include pension, profit sharing, and 401(k) plans; deferred compensation or executive retirement plans; supplemental life and disability insurance; stock options or phantom stock plans; and performance-related bonus plans.

But if I enhance benefits for key employees, don't I have to do it for everyone?

Many business owners feel that, in order to develop attractive compensation packages to retain their top managers, they need to increase compensation for all employees across the board. Fortunately, this is not true.

Group benefits and qualified plans *are* subject to limitations and strict non-discrimination rules, and must be offered to *all* employees. They are 100% tax deductible by the company.

Non-qualified plans, on the other hand, allow you to provide benefits for selected key employees—and for yourself—on a discriminatory basis. Depending on the benefit, it may be necessary to include all employees of a given class or classes of employees. But for some benefits, you can simply pick and choose the individuals you wish to include. In some cases, the costs are deductible currently; in others (supplemental retirement plans, for example), tax deductions are deferred until the benefit is paid. Funding is generally optional, but highly recommended. There are a number of funding methods available to employers, including mutual funds, stocks, bonds, life insurance, and disability insurance. The insurance alternatives avoid current earnings taxation and can often provide cost recovery to the corporation.

"Golden Handcuffs"

Non-qualified executive benefits plans are often referred to as "golden handcuffs" plans. Because the benefits are not immediately realized, the employee is bound to the company by the promise of future reward. But the valuable nature of the benefits makes that bond a "golden" one.

Golden handcuffs plans are designed to reward and retain top employees, and to provide an incentive for continued loyalty and high performance. These benefits are often extended to business owners as well, providing additional financial security at the corporation's expense rather than the owner's personal expense.

A secure financial foundation for business owners or executives includes:

- **Disability insurance.** What happens if you suffer a long-term or permanent disability? Will you be able to support yourself and your family? Will you be forced to deplete your assets when you are no longer able to earn an income?

- **Life insurance.** In the event of your death, what will happen to your family? Where will their income come from? Will their standard of living decrease? Will they still be able to afford educational, medical, and other expenses?

- **Retirement plans.** Will you have enough money to retire when you wish, and still maintain your standard of living?

Your company may already offer these benefits to all employees. Perhaps you already have group life and disability programs, as well as a pension plan, 401(k), or other retirement plans.

Shouldn't these benefits be sufficient for my top managers?

You may be surprised to learn that these types of standard group benefits actually provide *less* benefits for your top managers than they do for your regular employees.

Reverse Discrimination

Top executives will naturally be more highly compensated than your other employees. Surprisingly, this fact often works *against* them when it comes to group benefits. Most group benefits have limitations or benefit caps which result in *reverse discrimination*: the coverage provided is actually lower, percentage-wise, for executives than it is for employees. As a result, these benefits are often insufficient to meet executives' needs. For example:

- **Disability insurance.** Most group disability plans have a benefit cap. A typical plan may replace 60% of the employee's monthly salary, up to a maximum amount (let's say $3,000 per month). The $3,000 cap means that employees earning up to $60,000 per year ($5,000 per month) will have the full 60% of their salary replaced. Employees earning more than $60,000 annually, or whose compensation includes a bonus, will receive a smaller percentage of their salary. For example, an executive earning $100,000 per year will only have 36% of his or her salary replaced. This could result in severe financial strain and a significant drop in the executive's standard of living in the event of disability.

Reverse Discrimination: Disability Income Benefits		
	Employee	**Executive**
Annual salary	$40,000	$100,000
Monthly salary	$3,334	$8,333
Disability benefit	$2,000	$3,000
Percentage of income replaced	**60%**	**36%**

- **Life insurance.** Technically, there is no limit on the amount of group life insurance that can be offered to employees. However, employees must pay income tax on the "imputed economic benefit" of life insurance in excess of $50,000. The economic benefit is calculated according to the Internal Revenue Service's Table I rates, which range from 5¢ to $2.06 per *month*, per $1,000 of death benefit, depending on age. The high rates quickly defeat the "benefit" of additional life insurance.

  Life insurance is valuable to an employee because it can cover funeral expenses, pay off debts, and provide needed income to the employee's family. However, just as with disability insurance, there is a difference, percentage-wise, in how much value the benefit may actually provide to an employee. While $50,000 may be a significant amount to the family of a worker who earns $25,000 a year, it may not seem like much to the family of an executive whose combined annual salary and bonus is $200,000.

- **Retirement plans.** Retirement income has become a major concern for most individuals. Because people are living longer, they require retirement income for longer periods of time. With the future of Social Security uncertain, employees are looking for ways to ensure that they have enough money to maintain their standard of living through their later years.

  Corporate retirement plans (such as pension, profit sharing, and 401(k) plans) as well as individual retirement plans (IRAs, Simplified Employee Pension, and Keogh plans) have contribution limits which discriminate against more highly compensated individuals. For example, in 1998 the maximum allowable contribution to a 401(k) plan was $10,000. This allows an employee earning $40,000 a year to contribute up to 25% of salary. This same $10,000 limit, however, means that an executive earning $200,000 annually can contribute only 5%. There are similar limitations on other types of qualified plans, such as profit sharing and money purchase pension plans. For example:

Maximum Annual Retirement Plan Contributions		Employee	Executive
Annual Salary		$40,000	$200,000*
Profit Sharing Plan	Maximum	$ 6,000	$ 24,000
	Percentage of Salary	15%	12%
Money Purchase Plan	Maximum	$ 4,000	$ 16,000
	Percentage of Salary	10%	8%
401(k) Plan	Maximum	$10,000	$10,000
	Percentage of Salary	25%	5%

*According to IRS rules, allowable compensation is capped at $160,000 for contributions to profit sharing and pension plan accounts (15% x $160,000 = $24,000 for profit sharing; 10% x $160,000 = $16,000 for pension.)

It's clear from these examples that your key employees—who are generally also your highly compensated employees—do not necessarily receive a significant advantage from the standard group benefits offered by most companies.

To provide an attractive executive compensation package, a business owner must find more creative and cost-effective ways to offer employee benefits that are valuable—and appreciated. A number of non-qualified plans, which can be offered on a discriminatory basis, provide the best solution to this problem. Such plans include:

- supplemental disability programs;
- long-term care programs;
- supplemental life insurance;
- split-dollar life insurance;
- deferred compensation;
- 401(k) "top hat" plans;
- supplemental retirement plans;

- phantom stock option plans; and
- reverse split-dollar plans.

Okay, let's say I've got my key people "handcuffed." But I don't want to lose **anyone.** *There are some wonderful people in the rank and file who've been with me for decades.*

It's wonderful that you want to be sure they're taken care of, too. I'll assume you already have some form of group benefits program in place, but let's begin at the beginning anyway. Here are some questions you need to ask yourself:

Does my current group benefits plan...

- consistently meet my company's budget goals?
- provide my employees with the types of benefits that they really want...and need?
- take maximum advantage of the tax code and utilize the most innovative products and services available in the marketplace?
- provide a level of benefits that is competitive within the industry?

Does my current group benefits provider...

- offer accurate, prompt, courteous service?
- provide flexibility in plan design, funding, and administration?
- extend the lowest possible rates and fees?
- resolve problems quickly and efficiently?

I'll be honest with you...I **think** *the answer to each one of those questions is "yes," but don't quote me.*

That's understandable. But remember, we're talking about preparing your company to continue running smoothly *without* you—perhaps even *more* smoothly. So with that in mind, consider that a good benefits program should:

- address both your company's goals and your employees' needs.
- provide comprehensive and flexible benefits within your company's budget.

- provide a competitive level of benefits relative to other companies in your field.
- work as an incentive to allow you to attract and retain top-quality employees and executives.
- be clearly understood and appreciated by both management and employees.
- build employee morale and loyalty.
- generate increased employee dedication and productivity.
- be regularly re-evaluated to ensure that it is meeting your needs.

You listed the types of non-qualified benefits that should be included in an executive benefits package. But what types of benefits should be included in the benefits package we offer to all employees?

In today's competitive market, you should offer your employees a comprehensive benefits package that includes:

- group medical, prescription, dental, vision, and hearing coverage;
- group disability and life insurance;
- health care and dependent care flexible spending accounts;
- profit sharing and 401(k) plans; and
- defined benefit pension plans.

But my accounting manager advises me that our benefits program already adds something like 25 or 30% to our payroll costs.

Which is why you want to put benefit dollars to work *efficiently*. For example, if you are administering any of your plans internally, consider carefully whether you should continue to do so. Your company may not have the expertise or the technology to process the mountain of updated regulatory information that's generated every year, to say nothing of directing your contributions into the right investment options.

You should have a comprehensive benefits program that's custom-designed to generate the highest degree of dedication and productivity from *all* of your employees. And, you'll want to have it re-evaluated regularly to make sure it remains competitive and cost-effective.

Just like we re-evaluate our employees regularly.

Exactly.

Chapter Summary

- Your successor will not play the only important role in the future of your company. Key executives, managers, and employees are just as important to the operation of your business.

- In today's highly competitive marketplace, good employees are harder to find and retain.

- A top priority of any business owner should be to develop a compensation package that is (1) competitive within the industry, and (2) provides valuable benefits to attract and retain high-quality employees.

- Retaining good employees is an important concern throughout the life of a company, but it is especially critical during the transition period when an owner leaves the company and his or her successor takes over. Employees may feel a good deal of uncertainty about the company and their futures within it.

- Two obvious answers to enhancing compensation are increased salaries and/or additional or enhanced group benefits. However:

  - salary increases (with their attendant increased taxes) can be cost-prohibitive for the company. In addition, they provide an immediate benefit to employees that may not provide an incentive to stay on in the future.

  - enhanced group benefits must be offered to *all* employees, which may also be cost-prohibitive to the company.

- Benefit caps and limitations often result in *reverse discrimination* against highly compensated owners and executives, making these benefits ineffective for their needs. *Reverse discrimination* means that the benefit provided is actually lower, percentage-wise, for highly compensated executives than it is for rank and file employees.

- The best incentives are those that provide employees with a future benefit, encouraging them to stay with the company to realize a later reward.

- Executive benefits can be provided in a cost-effective manner through non-qualified plans. Such plans can be offered on a discriminatory basis to specific employees.

6

Ownership Succession

"I was expecting this, but not so soon."

—Boot Hill, Arizona
Tombstone Inscription

None of us has a crystal ball that tells us how our future will unfold. But we need to be as prepared as we can for unforeseen situations, both big and small, that are certain to arise. For example, if something were to happen to you, who's got the key to that file drawer in your office credenza? Who knows how to reach your biggest supplier on Sunday? Who best remembers which clients to contact on important dates?

In short, how much of the minutiae of your business is in your head? And what provisions have you made to pass *it* to your successors along with the deed to the store?

Ownership succession, if not well planned in advance, can be—at best—a difficult, lengthy, and expensive process. At worst, your company may be doomed as another statistic in the "70 per cent column" of family businesses that don't survive into the second generation.

The first responsibility of ownership, therefore, may be the responsibility of ensuring—and *insuring*—that the business survives your departure, whether through death, disability, or retirement.

Well, fine. First thing tomorrow I'll give my secretary a key to the file drawer. Good enough?

Only if you're leaving the firm to her. Remember, when you founded the business, you were the "chief cook and bottle washer." Chances are, you've relinquished that role, and many of your other original duties. Today, you've got upper management. You've got middle management. You've got specialists. And you've got *responsibilities of ownership*.

The Eight Functions of Business

- Executive
- Administrative
- Finance
- Marketing
- Product Knowledge
- Quality Control
- Research and Development
- Communications and Technology

Have you identified these eight functions in *your* business? Are responsibilities given to the right people with "the right stuff"? And are they adequately prepared to take over for you—especially on short notice?

Well, those are good questions. And the answers are "I think so," "I hope so," and "I'm not so sure anymore."

Fine. That's a start. Now here's another question: is the person(s) you designate as your successor prepared to assume their *own* responsibilities of ownership?

I don't understand. What will they have to do differently from what I do today? After all, it's the same company.

Is it? When you leave it through retirement—and then pass it to your heirs when you die—the pie may still be apple, but it'll be cut up in a whole new way. Read on:

> *Mr. Founder began his business in the 1920s. He did not formulate a succession plan, so upon his death, two of his sons—Sam and Joey—and his son-in-law Tom take over the company. Sam's son and son-in-law work for the firm; Joey and Tom have no children. A buy-sell agreement is drawn up whereby Sam's interest will be bought out by his son and son-*

in-law upon his death, and the corporation will pay Joey's and Tom's estates for their shares. Each buy-out was more than adequately funded by life insurance products.

Then...fate takes over. Of the three second-generation owners, Joey passes away first. The agreement is re-structured so that Sam's son and son-in-law will buy out Sam's and Tom's interest. They do so upon Tom's death in his early seventies, and Sam's at age eighty.

Sam's son-in-law decides to leave the business. His interest is bought out by Sam's son, who now has a daughter—the fourth generation, if you're keeping score at home—waiting in the wings to head up a firm now worth some $30 million.

Point #1: All plans were in place, all funding was in place, and all families are financially secure, with minimal taxation.

Point #2: Great-granddaughter will inherit a company that's far removed in every way from Mr. Founder's business begun seventy years earlier.

So you want me to plan today for the year 2070? Excuse me, but I've got a stack of messages this high from customers right now, and if I don't make them happy, there won't be a business for me, never mind for a great-granddaughter I don't have yet.

That's the whole point right there. Nobody's saying to you, "Ms. Busy Business Owner, forget about your clients and write up those buy-sell agreements."

What we *are* suggesting is, begin thinking about and planning for the future *with the help of your advisors whom you pay to advise you!* And here's where to start.

Objectives in Transferring Ownership

- Income for the Owner/Spouse
- Tax Savings
- Meeting Personal Goals

You wouldn't mount a video camcorder on a stand with only two legs; it wouldn't stand for long. A stand with four legs won't work on uneven surfaces, such as hills. That's why some enterprising photographer invented the tripod. With three legs of adjustable lengths, your camcorder is supported so it can function under any conditions.

And so it is with your business.

If you're the head of a large, public company, you have a legal department, an accounting department, and a finance department. If you own a closely held or family business, you retain an attorney and a CPA, but chances are you don't employ a dedicated person to handle your corporate and personal *financial* affairs.

Working through your attorney and your CPA, you need to get the third member of the triad on board: a *specialist* in financial and business succession planning.

If you needed heart surgery, you wouldn't ask your family doctor to do the job. You'd seek a qualified cardiac surgeon. The same concept applies to financial and business succession planning. A qualified specialist's background, experience, and skill can provide significant advantages.

You're right—I like these advantages. Let's talk about the first objective in transferring ownership, "Income for the Owner/Spouse." What do I have to do to gain this advantage?

Get Both of Your Houses in Order

Realize right now that, as a business owner, part of your business plan is inexorably linked to your personal plan. Your grand scheme for the business must consider your strategies for home and family. It must also consider these questions:

- Can you convert the business into a stream of income without jeopardizing your security?
- Do you have income sources outside of the business?
- Where will your post-retirement income come from?
- Do you have an estate plan?

Get Your Brain Picked Now

If you remember nothing else in this book, please remember this:

No one can pick your brain after you die!

It's vital that you make your wishes known. Your current and future objectives—both business *and* personal—must be discussed before your business succession plan can be finalized. Ask yourself these questions:

- Have I created vision and mission statements for the business? Are my successors familiar with them? Are they committed to them?
- Are my key employees aware of my strategic plan?
- Do I have a successor in mind? If so, do the right people know who it is?

- Have I developed a short-term strategic contingency plan in case I suddenly die or become disabled? If so, do my key people know that it exists? Do they know where to find it?

Don't just *address* these issues: *communicate* them—to your spouse, your heirs, and your key employees. Taking for granted that people know what you want can result in confusion, resentment, and even financial disaster.

Get Junior Plugged In

The responsibilities of business ownership will be passed on along with the ownership itself. Are your successors ready? Do they know what to expect behind the "big" desk? Are they equipped to handle the multitude of responsibilities that come with the territory?

Once a succession plan is in place, your successors must be meticulously trained, and even put through simulations like a "Top Gun" pilot.

And while all this is going on, part of the plan must be to *get the successor's house in order, too!*

Let's say your successor is your son. Does Junior have an estate plan? Has he provided for the financial security of his family? Does he have a contingency plan? If not, he should start *now*, while it's less expensive to fund the necessary financial vehicles.

By addressing these issues, you can be sure that your (and your spouse's) income stream will be protected after you retire.

Now, about that "Tax Savings" objective you mentioned. How can I control the tax situation?

Let's consider Junior again. If you'll be selling your business to him—or to a group of family members—you're not necessarily looking for the highest sales price for your equity. Your priorities are (1) the highest degree of security, and (2) the lowest rate of taxation. If you're selling to an outside party your goal is to get as high a price as possible, but this strategy can have the negative effect of increasing your capital gains tax and subsequent estate tax. Similarly, if you're not around to set a modest selling price when your heirs are ready to buy the business, the IRS will be happy to assign a high value to it so they can collect maximum estate taxes, thus forcing a conclusion you don't want.

Control your own destiny. Make your *own* decisions. Which is to say, take action while you're still empowered to do so. Consider this example:

> *A father sells a business to his son for $10 million. A ten-year note gives Dad and Son the security they each need, and provides Dad with some voting shares along with it. Dad's capital gains tax is payable at a reduced rate due to the length of the payout. And although Son can't deduct the payments, the business has now been valued and all future appreciation will be outside Dad's estate. This is especially helpful since Son already has an offer to purchase for double the $10 million he just paid. Dad's decision to sell the business to his son during his lifetime will save a fortune in estate taxes.*

Later, we will explore techniques for "gifting" the business and keeping the legacy intact.

And finally, what about the last objective: "Meeting Personal Goals"?

Again, the key word is *security*. You want your present *and future* income secured, and your spouse's sources of income likewise secured. Your goals may also include fair equalization of your estate for those members of your family who are not directly involved in the succession of the business.

Finally, you want to be sure that top management is comfortable with your plans, as they have, quite literally, a "vested interest" in the company's future, whether you're a part of it or not.

Yes, but what about my vested interest in how the company is run? My way of doing business may conflict with that of my successor or the Board of Directors. Can I guarantee that the philosophy on which the firm was founded will continue in my absence?

Probably no more than you can require your employees to use typewriters instead of word processing computers just because *you* still use one. Change and progress are going to happen, with or without you.

That said, we've already mentioned vision and mission statements. If you don't have them, draft them. Post them in the lobby, in the lunchroom, in the boardroom. Let them come from your heart, and instill them into the heart of your successors.

If you'll be succeeded exclusively by family members, you might want to get together to draft family vision and mission statements: a series of ideals, policies, guidelines, and rules for the continuance of the business as part of the larger "organization" that is your family.

Owner Exit Strategies

So you've finally decided. You're taking the "And Son" sign you had made when he was born, and are now ready to hammer it up there on the storefront along with your own name. At the same time, you and your spouse are packing, and you'll decide where you're going later.

Okay, so maybe that's a little dramatic. Nevertheless, you've made the decision to leave while the decision is still yours to make. Now: how to do it? Or, to continue the dramatic metaphor, how to exit, stage right, while the applause is still ringing in the rafters?

In Chapter 2, we touched on the four "owner exit strategies." Let's review them briefly.

Liquidation

Liquidation is usually, and tragically, the end result of a lack of planning. And in the end, the liquidators come in, take everything, and give you next to nothing for it.

If you find yourself on this road with no room to make a U-turn, you can at least pull off to the side and contact someone in the industry who may be interested in your inventory. If you're in the restaurant business or have a medical practice, for example, you may well find someone who would pay more for the equipment through a direct sale than you'd get by selling to a liquidator.

Start planning today.

Sale to an Outside Party

Wait a minute! I told you before, I've got kids and good people waiting to take the reins. Why would I sell to an outsider?

Maybe *you* wouldn't. But many owners do, for as many reasons as there are owners. Simply put, many of them just "want out" after a professional lifetime of going to the shop every morning, and taking the shop's problems home every evening. And unlike you, they may have no one in the wings willing—or able—to continue on.

So they go looking for a buyer. And *that's* where that lifetime of work can quickly and very literally become dramatically devalued.

Let me guess...they make the mistake of trying to do it themselves.

Exactly. Don't look for a *buyer*—look for someone who can find a buyer *for* you! And as we've discussed, that person should be someone in the "looking for a buyer" business, a specialist with experience and objectivity who will work on your behalf but not be straight-jacketed by current or previous ties to you or your company.

An investment banker, business broker, or other consultant should handle the task of packaging the firm and its assets for sale. Each has different strengths and areas of specialization; investigate each proposal thoroughly before proceeding, as you would any transaction. The stakes are obvious.

Then what?

Agree on how the sale should be structured. Your advisors will raise questions and suggest strategies, such as:

- What is the asking price, and what are the terms?
- What is the financial status of the prospective buyer?
- Will this be a sale of assets or of stock?
- Is it to your benefit to opt for a tax-free sale (or stock swap)?

Each strategy will, of course, come with its own set of positive and negative aspects. Most critical, however, are the tax implications.

Selling the family business to a third party can be stressful. A comparison to selling one's own child would not be totally out of line, as many business owners nurture their companies as tenderly as a cherished child.

The best advice I can give you to minimize the stress of selling is to *prepare for the sale in advance*. When you decide to sell your house, what's the first thing you do? You prepare for the sale by fixing it up. You don't want to have to settle for less money because the house needs minor repairs.

Similarly, you don't want your family business to be regarded as a "fixer-upper" by a prospective buyer. So get your "house" in order: have the financial records audited and the business appraised as soon as feasible. In some cases, this happens *years* before the eventual sale.

And don't fret! What may have been originally approached as the "end of an era" may well turn out to be the beginning of an even better one.

Sale to Family or Employees

The techniques and options associated with this strategy are numerous, and will be covered in the next three chapters.

Gifting

I'm glad we left this option for last. As a businessman, I understand all about "selling." I don't understand the advantages of "giving." How does this benefit me?

How's this for an advantage: another generation of existence for your business. Gifting—either during your lifetime or through your estate—has the potential for an exciting variety of tax-saving applications.

Detailed information on gifting is included in Chapters 10 and 15.

Chapter Summary

- The first responsibility of ownership may be the responsibility of ensuring—and *insuring*—that the business survives your departure.
- Ask yourself:
  - Have I identified the eight functions of business as they apply to *my* company?
  - Have I delegated the right responsibilities to the right people?
  - Are these people adequately prepared to take over, especially on short notice?
- Begin thinking about and planning for the future with your advisors. Objectives in transferring ownership include:
  - income for the owner/spouse,
  - tax savings, and
  - meeting personal goals.
- Working with your attorney and CPA, bring the remaining member of your "advisor triad" on board: a financial advisor specializing in estate and business succession planning.
- Efficient business succession is the result of preparing for—and properly executing—one of the four owner exit strategies:
  - liquidation,
  - sale to an outside party,
  - sale to family or employees, or
  - gifting.

7

Selling the Business

"Few men of action have been able to make a
graceful exit at the appropriate time."

—Malcolm Muggeridge, 1903-90
English Editor and Writer

It goes without saying that selling a business is more complex, with more pitfalls and cracks in the system to fall through, than selling a house. Even so, there are still just three basic steps to put you on the right path towards closing the deal: (1) establishing a value for your business, (2) agreeing on a price, and (3) agreeing on the method of transaction.

Failure to plan an orderly transition of the company can have catastrophic results:

- If you don't arrange for a buyer to purchase the business upon your death, your surviving spouse may not have adequate cash flow to maintain your accustomed standard of living.

- Estate tax liabilities could force liquidation of the business.

To avoid such financial disasters, you should create—and periodically update—a *buy/sell agreement*.

How?

Establish a value for your business that will satisfy both the IRS and your minority shareholders. Then, decide who will buy the business upon your death, what price will be paid, and what type of buy/sell agreement will be transacted.

Having a buy/sell agreement in place can make huge lifestyle differences for your surviving spouse and family. Consider the following case:

> *Moe and Joe, who had been brother-partners for years, had no buy/sell agreement between them. Ever since Moe died twenty years ago, Joe has been running the business, carefully guiding it through the ups and downs that all businesses experience. Moe's widow, with no interest or skill for the task, has nevertheless retained her bequeathed stock and has become an equal and vocal partner in all decisions: hiring and firing, bonuses, profit sharing distributions, and expenditures of funds. Now Joe's son wants to join the business, but Mrs. Moe says no.*
>
> *If there had been a cross-purchase agreement funded with life insurance which provided that one partner could buy the other's half of the company upon his death, Joe would have been able to buy Moe's share when he died. Mrs. Moe would have been financially secure—and out of the business—twenty years earlier.*

What kind of buy/sell agreement should I use?

There are two types of buy/sell agreements: cross-purchase agreements and stock redemption agreements.

Cross-Purchase Agreement

A cross-purchase agreement occurs when stock is sold directly from the owner to a buyer, such as a child or a partner. The company as an entity is not a party to this transaction.

Sounds easy enough. My daughter buys my shares and I'm out of there.

It *is* easy. But we should discuss the tax implications. A cross-purchase agreement offers a number of advantages. The most significant is a step-up in basis on the stock. That is, in the event of a sale down the road—your daughter to *her* daughter, for example—the transaction for tax purposes begins with the price your daughter paid you for her interest. If insurance proceeds are used to fund the agreement, they are not subject to an alternative minimum tax, nor are they subject to seizure by creditors.

Be advised, however, that a lifetime sale is taxable to you as a capital gain, above and beyond the cost you paid for the business, and that the purchase price is not a deductible expense to the buyer.

Also, if there is more than one buyer—or seller, for that matter—this type of agreement becomes more complicated. However, it is much better to sort these issues out now than to leave them for your advisors and family.

Stock Redemption Agreement

A stock redemption transaction is accomplished by selling your stock back to the corporation. The redeemed shares are retired, and the remaining shareholders own 100% of the company. This can be done either by you or by your estate.

Tax considerations in stock redemption agreements are similar to those in cross-purchase agreements in that a lifetime sale is taxable to the seller (above cost basis), and the amount paid by the buyer—whether paid in a lump sum or spread out over time—is not deductible.

The corporation, however—unlike an individual buyer—may be subject to an alternative minimum tax on life insurance proceeds used to fund the agreement because the corporation is the owner and beneficiary of the policy. Also, insurance proceeds in this case are subject to creditor claims.

And, there is another potential pitfall inherent with a stock redemption agreement (but not with a cross-purchase agreement).

What's that?

It's called *attribution*, a situation in which surviving family members are liable for income taxes on the stock redemption. This happens when the family members are also stockholders, thus receiving the indirect benefit of an increase in ownership when the redemption occurs. (Attribution is spelled out in detail in Section 318 of the Internal Revenue Code.) Generally, to avoid creating a family attribution situation, you can use a cross-purchase agreement. It's critically important that you discuss attribution with your tax advisors prior to any transaction.

How often should buy/sell agreements be revised?

It depends, but all agreements should be updated periodically. Things happen; family situations change. For example…

> Brothers Harvey, Jimmy, and Bob were in business together. They drew up a stock redemption agreement many years ago. Over the years, each brother had children who came into the business. Harvey passed away first. Under the provisions of the agreement, Jimmy and Bob acquired Harvey's stock. The result? Harvey's child ended up as an employee working for his cousins, the victim of "Russian Roulette" as to which brother would die first.

Sounds like they needed a cross-purchase agreement.

Why?

That way Harvey's son would've inherited his father's interest.

Well, not inherit. A separate agreement set up between each father-and-child group would provide that the father's stock would be purchased by the child working in the business. Note that the balance of control of the company remains the same, so a cross-purchase agreement should also be considered by partners who are not blood relatives.

We talked about buy/sell agreements that are put into force as a retirement tool and those that become effective upon the owner's death. Can they be used in the event of disability?

Yes, absolutely. An agreement should be drafted, and then updated to include that eventuality. After all, of the three—retirement, death, and disability—the last is the least predictable.

Let's get off that subject, if it's okay. Tell me how I set a price for my business.

As we said, putting a value on your life's work is more complex than putting a sign on your front lawn. And yet, there are similarities.

Methods of Business Valuation

The value of any business is generally described as "fair market value." This is defined as the price a business would bring between a willing buyer and seller. But since closely held businesses are sold privately and the stock is not traded on an established exchange, it can be difficult to determine a "fair" value. In addition, the transaction may not encompass the entire business, but only one shareholder's interest. Nevertheless, a value must be determined—at the very least, for tax purposes.

The IRS has ruled that the following factors are basic determinants of a business' value:

1. The nature and history of the business.
2. The general economic forecast, and that of the specific industry into which the business falls.
3. The business' book value and its financial state.
4. Its earning capability.
5. Its ability to pay dividends.
6. Intangible values that may affect future earnings and, consequently, the asking price.
7. History of stock sales and the proportion of the business that is placed on the market.
8. Comparison with prices of companies that are similar but publicly traded.

Third-party valuation professionals—and there *are* such people—use a number of techniques. They'll tell you, however, that their profession is more art than science, and a final valuation may result from a combination—a "hybrid"—of the following methods.

Income Approach

- **Capitalized earnings.** This method estimates future earnings, and divides that figure by an investor's ideal rate of return. If a business earns $200,000 annually, and a rate of five times earnings (a 20% return) is standard for this industry, the business might be valued at $1 million.

- **Discounted future cash flow.** The future income and expenses of the business are calculated, and the value is then determined using a discounted rate of return on investment.

- **Discounted future earnings.** This is similar to the discounted cash flow method, but calculated on earnings rather than on income and expenses.

Market Approach

- **Similar private companies.** Information from recent sales of similar closely held companies is evaluated and adjusted for specifics of the individual company to derive a value.

- **Publicly traded companies.** Information such as price/earnings ratios on companies traded on exchanges may be used to estimate a value.

Asset Approach

- **Assets minus liabilities.** The "book value" of a business may be derived by as simple a method as subtracting its liabilities from its assets as indicated on financial records and current statements.

- **Liquidation appraisal.** This method discounts the book value to prepare for a "fire sale" of the company.

Since every company—and the sale of every company—is different, the asking price may, as noted above, be determined by using a combination of methods.

Hybrid Approach

- **Tangibles plus intangibles.** Since this method combines book value with the excess earnings method, it is considered a hybrid method. A goodwill value is determined and added to the value of the operating assets. To arrive at goodwill, the earnings of the business are compared with industry averages. Using factors developed by various reporting services, the excess over industry averages is computed. This excess is then multiplied by factors supplied by various industry guides. The appraisers may modify this figure based on their own experience and expertise to determine a goodwill amount. This amount is then added to the acquisition value of the assets (net of liabilities) to arrive at a total value.

- **Standards of the industry.** Appraisers may elect to use standard formulas to estimate a company's value. For example, if it's a retail business, they may use a multiple of earnings per square feet. *Estimate* is the key word here, as such standards are broad generalizations at best.

Available Discounts and Premiums

We've asserted that the sale of your business is more complex by far than selling a personal possession such as a house. There might be some validity, however, in stretching the comparison to include the sale of a product in the open market. If you're a dressmaker, you sell your goods wholesale to mass merchandisers, offering them deep discounts for volume purchases. At the same time, you take a fair markup, which is passed along to the retail buying public.

Discounts and markups (premiums) are a critical part of the valuation process, impacting both your ability to sell the company and the achievement of your personal goals in doing so. Discounts, in this regard, are usually given for two reasons: lack of marketability, and minority (non-controlling) interest.

Lack of Marketability Discount

Sure, you're able to sell your interest now, but what about the buyer's chances? How easy will it be to turn those shares over again? For one thing, they are illiquid in that they can't simply be redeemed on the open market. For another, the time that it takes to find a subsequent buyer may severely depress the resulting price.

The IRS recognizes this situation, and allows for a reasonable discount for lack of marketability, averaging 35%.

Minority Interest Discount

Put yourself in the place of the buyer. What's he or she getting—the whole company, or just one piece of the pie? And if it's the latter, how big is the piece? And what's that piece really worth when it comes to controlling the course that the business will take?

A 20% shareholder can certainly wield influence, but cannot exercise unilateral decision-making authority. Recognizing that a 20% interest in your company is not "worth" 20% of the company's total value or book value or whatever yardstick is used, a separate discount is allowed. Such a discount could be valued at another 20%...or more.

Controlling Interest Premium

Let's get back now to you as the seller. You might well argue, "If a non-controlling interest is discounted, shouldn't a *controlling* interest be marked up?" Yes, indeed.

A premium on majority-interest securities is allowable; the percentage varies depending on specific circumstances.

Voting and Non-Voting Shares

The price adjustments described above represent the sale of voting shares, discounted or marked up according to their perceived worth based on control and marketability.

Another technique is more a gifting issue than a selling tool, but warrants mention here. Your interest in the company, prior to its divestment, can be restructured into voting and non-voting shares.

If you desire a continued controlling interest in the company but wish to reduce your ownership position, you can retain voting shares and sell—or gift—*non-voting* shares. The sale of non-voting shares can also justify a discount.

> *Business owner Alice, now 70, sells 90% of her company to her son on a ten-year note. Before doing so, however, she converts the shares to non-voting shares. The agreement provides that the stock will reconvert to voting shares during the final year of the note. Alice has reduced her ownership to 10%, yet she retains full control over the company for the next nine years.*

If you are withdrawing from the company completely and only one of your children is active in the business, you can gift voting shares to the active child and non-voting shares to any inactive children.

Discounts, as they are used in the creation of family limited partnerships and limited liability companies, will be covered in Chapters 10 and 16.

Chapter Summary

- Selling a business can be broken down into three basic steps: establishing its value, agreeing on a price, and agreeing on the method of transaction.

- A *cross-purchase agreement* occurs when stock is sold directly from owner to buyer. It is uncomplicated (unless more than one buyer or seller is involved) and offers a number of tax advantages.

- A *stock redemption agreement* is accomplished by selling stock back to the corporation.

- Care should be taken to avoid the adverse tax consequences of *family attribution*.

- All buy-sell agreements should be periodically updated.

- Methods of business valuation can be grouped into *income*, *market*, and *asset approaches*. *Hybrid approaches* combine features of two or more of these.

- Discounts on business sales are given for two reasons: (1) when the stock has limited marketability, and (2) when the buyer is purchasing only a minority interest in the company.

- A premium may be charged for the sale of a controlling interest.

- Stockholders may convert their stock into voting and non-voting shares. Selling non-voting shares allows an owner to greatly reduce holdings while maintaining a controlling interest.

8

Funding the Buy/Sell Agreement

"An ounce of prevention is worth a pound of cure."

—Everyone's Grandmother

You've decided to sell your business, and you've wisely chosen anticipatory *pro*-action instead of a delayed *re*-action by formulating plans the easy way (now) instead of the hard way (later).

But how should you proceed? How should the buyout be structured? And what are the hurdles? For example, do you take a lump sum now and pay a one-time but potentially large capital gains tax, or do you spread the payments out over a period of time and pay the tax as you go along?

As you might suspect, there is no simple template—no "proper" method for transferring your business. The road you choose will depend in great measure on your financial status outside the business. What other sources of income do you have now? What about after the sale? How much money do you need immediately? Does that need outweigh the tax consequences of a lump sum sale?

Okay, let's take me, for instance. I've got children in the business I want to sell it to, and for their sake, I'd like to set the lowest price possible. I have enough other assets so I don't need the proceeds in a lump sum, but I can probably handle the taxes if we decide to go that route. What do I need to think about?

We've already discussed valuation, but again, bear in mind that your asking price must be deemed reasonable by the IRS for federal estate tax purposes. Low-balling the price for your children's sake may be frowned on by Uncle Sam. That being the case, you can guess the result.

Gift taxes?

Yes, gift taxes—on the difference between your eventual selling price and what the IRS feels the business is actually worth.

So how do I comply with their idea of what's reasonable?

Oddly enough, this requirement may not prove to be that difficult to meet. Presenting a case history of a similar business and its selling price, for example, may be enough. If you've received a recent offer from an outside buyer, that may be acceptable proof of a reasonable valuation on your part. You must use some sort of valuation formula—a benchmark—that complies with the 1990 Tax Act, as opposed to setting an artificially low price for the family's sake.

An up-to-date business appraisal by a non-prejudicial source will, of course, be among the most required and most heavily weighted factors.

Is there a way I can legitimately reduce the value of the business for purposes of selling it to my children?

One way is to break the business up into smaller parts. For example, a "C" corporation may be restructured as a *family limited partnership*. Discounts of 20 to 40% may be realized due to the resulting lack of marketability and the creation of minority interests. (See Chapters 10 and 16.)

So—bottom line—what do I need to be thinking about today?

You and your spouse need to sit down and say, "Here's the value of our business. If we do nothing, our children will lose 55% of it to taxes when we die. We want them to have the business without having to take such a huge financial loss. What are some creative options we can use to transfer the company to our children and avoid having to deal with valuation and tax issues 10 or 20 years from now?"

And *that's* the bottom line.

Tell me about options for funding a business transfer.

The first, and least attractive, option is to let your heirs figure things out for themselves after you die—a sort of "pay-as-you-go" program. I'll assume—because you're reading this book—that you're not interested in this "no-plan" type of plan.

Second, your heirs could secure bank loans after your death. At that point in time, however, the borrowers must assume obligations to repay principal and interest, all without your continuance in the business to contribute toward the purchase price.

Let's take a look at Cynthia and Marie's situation:

> *Business partners Cynthia and Marie have no life insurance policies on each other. When Cynthia dies, Marie is overwhelmed. Without the help of her partner, she struggles to pay her own salary and benefits as usual,* and *to make payments on a bank loan she must take out to buy Cynthia's half of the company from her heirs. And because the transaction is an after-tax purchase, Marie can't even deduct the loan payments.*

> *And now for the bad news: Cynthia's heirs may not be willing to sell to Marie. Because the partners didn't have an agreement that spells out what will happen to the company when one of them dies, Cynthia's heirs could decide they don't want to give up their half of the business, and Marie could reluctantly find herself working with several new business partners.*

A third possible source of capital would be to establish a *sinking investment fund* while you're living. This can be a corporate asset in which you invest in equities, real estate, mutual funds, etc. The fund—hopefully—grows and remains liquid.

The problem with this approach, however—as with others we've discussed—is the "fortuneteller factor." None of us knows when we'll need ready cash to pay for the unexpected. Chances are, the fund won't have sufficient assets when you need it. Beyond that, the business will be liable for taxes on all of the income, dividends, and capital gains the fund earns. Lastly, as a practical matter, such funds—if they're liquid—can be siphoned off for other purposes along the way and may no longer be available for their original intent.

A fourth—and decidedly best—option for making sure money is available for business transfer at the owner's death is to create a buy/sell agreement and fund it with life insurance. The reasons are many and sound. Among them:

1. Life insurance proceeds are not typically subject to income taxes.

2. The proceeds can be structured to be estate tax-free, as well.

3. Proceeds are paid immediately, right when they're needed.

4. There is great leverage with life insurance, which provides the money needed for only pennies on the dollar.

Insurance is a disciplined investment that provides unsurpassed leverage. But best of all, it works like a contingency umbrella that covers you when you least expect the need to arise, whether it's due to death or disability. Fred's case is a perfect example:

> *Upon his death, Fred would like his children to be able to buy the business from Pauline, his wife. The purchase price is $1 million; the company is in the 34% tax bracket. Pauline wants $100,000 a year for ten years, plus interest. If the children do nothing to pay for the transfer, they will end up needing approximately $1,350,000 to fund the $1 million buyout!*

> *On top of that, the new owners of the business— Fred and Pauline's own children, remember—will have had to earn that money and pay applicable taxes on it. In order to net the average $135,000 annual payment, they would have to gross an average of some $185,000 a year…almost $2 million in earnings just to meet the $1 million selling price!*

> *But if the children spend perhaps $24,000 a year to buy a $1 million life insurance policy while Fred is*

> alive (assuming the policy is purchased when Fred is
> 60 years old), they could provide both of their
> parents with peace of mind—and themselves a
> guarantee that the purchase price will be paid in
> full *with* tax-free dollars!

Fred and his family would do well, indeed, to plan ahead.

Okay, so I need to create a buy/sell agreement, and I need to buy life insurance. But how do I set everything up to make sure my plan works the way I want?

We've seen that buy/sell agreements can be structured as cross-purchase or stock redemption agreements as methods of transfer. Let's look at how using life insurance as a funding vehicle can work for both of these types of agreements.

In the case of a stock redemption agreement, a life insurance policy is purchased on the owner's life. The corporation is the owner and the beneficiary of the policy and the proceeds are used to redeem the owner's stock from his or her estate. Generally, such an agreement is not appropriate for the transfer of assets between parent and child(ren).

A cross-purchase agreement is generally the best plan for family members because it avoids family attribution rules that may result in income taxes on the redemption of stock at the time of the owner's death. In a cross-purchase agreement, the child (or a trust) owns an insurance policy on the owner's life, but there is a stipulation that requires the death benefit to be paid to the owner's spouse in exchange for his or her interest in the company.

Let's say I have a buy/sell agreement with my brother, and we have life insurance on each other. Now my daughter wants to come into the business. What should we do with the insurance policies?

If you transfer ownership of the policy to your daughter, a potential complication may result under IRS "transfer-for-value" rules. This could cause her to be liable for income taxes on the proceeds.

There are some exceptions to the transfer-for-value rule. For example, if a father was also a partner in a limited partnership with his daughter, the corporate policy could be transferred to the partnership with no income tax due at time of death.

The following chart illustrates the transfer-for-value rule:

Transfer-for-Value Rule	
Transferee for Value	**Tax Result**
Insured	Exempt
Partner of insured	Exempt
Partnership in which insured is a partner	Exempt
Corporation in which insured is a shareholder or officer	Exempt
Anyone where basis is determined by reference to transferor's basis	Exempt
Co-stockholder of insured	Taxable
Spouse of insured (not incident to divorce)	Taxable
Anyone else	Taxable

Life insurance intended to fund a buy/sell agreement will be most valuable if it's drafted in the most tax-advantaged ways possible by an advisor experienced in this very specialized field.

What about funding for a sale prior to retirement?

There are a couple of ways to do this. You could set up a sinking fund—like the one I discussed earlier—invested in mutual funds or stocks, but there's still the problem of current taxation to the corporation on dividends and gains. A better way would be to fund a living buyout with the same vehicle you're using to fund the death buyout—namely, *life insurance*. The cash value growth in a life insurance policy is not subject to current taxation. And with today's creative products, your range of investment choices for the cash value is as varied as the stock market (with choices in large cap growth and value funds, international funds, etc.).

The cash value of the policy can be accessed at retirement (or before, if need be) with certain tax advantages. For example, withdrawals up to basis are tax-free. Cash value in excess of basis is also available tax-free via very low cost policy loans. The point here is that there are ways of combining a death benefit buyout with a living buyout using life insurance as a funding vehicle.

Chapter Summary

- There is no "proper" way to sell a business. Many factors—including your financial status outside the business—affect the way you should structure the transaction.

- Valuation of the business must comply with the Tax Act of 1990, and should include an up-to-date appraisal by an objective source. One way to legitimately reduce the value of a business is to break it up into smaller parts through a *family limited partnership*.

- Sources of funds include *pay-as-you-go, bank loans, sinking investment funds*, and *insurance*. Each has characteristics, both pro and con, which must be weighed carefully.

- A buy/sell agreement drafted prior to the owner's death provides for an orderly, less painful transfer. Using life insurance to fund the agreement offers many advantages:

  - proceeds are not typically subject to income taxes;
  - they may be estate tax-free, as well;
  - benefits are payable when they are most needed; and
  - proceeds are leveraged, letting you effectively fund the agreement with discounted dollars.

- Buy/sell agreements may be structured as *cross-purchase* or *stock redemption agreements* as methods of transfer during the owner's lifetime or at death. Cross-purchase agreements are generally best when family members are involved.

- Changing the ownership of insurance policies must be done carefully to avoid taxation under transfer-for-value rules.

9

Selling the Company to Your Employees: The ESOP

"Effective managers live in the present—but concentrate on the future."

—James L. Hayes, 1895-1971
President and CEO
American Management Association

An *employee stock ownership plan* (or "ESOP") is a qualified employer plan—similar to a profit sharing plan—in which participants' funds are invested in stock of the employer company. Like a standard profit sharing plan, a percentage of each employee's salary is contributed to the ESOP. The difference is, because these contributions are invested back into the company itself, an ESOP—at least in theory—increases employee loyalty, commitment, and productivity.

What kinds of companies establish ESOPs?

Ideal ESOP candidates meet a majority of the following criteria:

- The company's owner is looking to "cash out" all or part of his or her stock.
- The company is closely held rather than publicly traded. Publicly traded companies can establish ESOPs, but there are certain drawbacks (such as, all shareholders must be allowed to vote their stock).
- The company has a strong earnings or cash flow record over the last five years.

- One or more stockholders is interested in a tax-advantaged means of selling some of their stock.

- Shareholders are willing to share partial (possibly minority) ownership with employees.

- A strong management team is ready to take over if a principal leaves the company.

- The company currently makes payments to a profit sharing or other qualified plan that could be diverted into an ESOP.

- The company expects to pay substantial federal income taxes over the next few years. (ESOPs can provide income tax deductions.)

What advantages does an ESOP offer to the selling shareholders and to the company?

ESOPs offer many attractive advantages, including:

- An ESOP allows shareholders to diversify their investments and increase liquidity without an immediate loss of control over the company.

- An ESOP creates a market for closely held stock that might not otherwise exist.

- Shareholders can defer or eliminate capital gains tax on the stock sold if the ESOP owns at least 30% of the corporate stock, and if the proceeds from stock sold to the ESOP are reinvested in domestic stocks and bonds within a specified time. If those securities are held until death, the shareholder's family gets a step-up in basis at death, so if they're sold at that time, there would be no capital gains taxes.

- In a leveraged ESOP, principal and interest payments on the ESOP loan are tax-deductible to the corporation.

- Dividends are tax-deductible to the corporation if they are passed on to employees or are used to reduce ESOP debt.

- Corporate contributions of stock or cash to the ESOP are tax-deductible.

- An ESOP can enhance corporate debt-carrying capacity and improve corporate cash flow because the employer can use it as a conduit for borrowing money from a bank or other financial institution.

- By providing employees with partial ownership of the company, an ESOP can act as an incentive to retain employees and improve morale and productivity.

Given these advantages, it sounds like an ESOP could be used to achieve a number of objectives.

You're right. Here are some of those objectives, and the types of companies that might use an ESOP to achieve them:

- private companies looking to solve succession and long-term planning issues;
- private companies whose owners wish to diversify their personal net worth while remaining in full operational control of the stock that is sold;
- private companies that want to recover the corporate income taxes paid in the prior three tax years;
- private companies seeking to acquire a competitor, supplier, or unrelated business with pre-tax dollars;
- management buy-out groups who would like to acquire their company with pre-tax dollars;
- private or public companies that wish to convert an existing pension or profit sharing plan from a "pure expense" item to one that increases shareholder equity, working capital, and cash flow; and
- public companies looking to privatize, expand shareholder base, divest a division, or create a friendly block of shareholders as a takeover defense measure.

A question about principal and interest payments on ESOP-based loans. Not that I'm complaining, mind you, but why are they tax-deductible?

Payments into an ESOP are treated as a contribution to a qualified plan. If a company earns $1 million of profits, it would normally have to pay $340,000 in taxes (being in the 34% bracket). If the company puts the $1million into an ESOP instead, and the ESOP repays the bank, the result is that the company has purchased a million-dollar loan for $660,000.

So if I sell $10 million in stock to a leveraged ESOP...

...you save up to $2 million in capital gains taxes, and the effective cost to the corporation is $6.6 million ($10 million tax deductible nets $6.6 million in a 34% corporate tax bracket). You save $2 million, and the corporation saves $3.4 million. That's a nice result.

By distributing stock to employees, aren't I giving up control of the company, share-by-share?

It would seem so. But in reality, you could maintain control of the company by retaining the right to choose the ESOP's trustees who, in most instances, will vote all corporate shares. In addition, if the plan provides for distribution of stock in kind, you retain the means of redeeming stock from the employees.

Here are two examples of how an ESOP can be a win-win situation, especially for a current owner(s) with some specific circumstances:

Example 1

Walter is the sole owner of a business worth $12 million. Unfortunately, he has no personal assets outside the business—it's his entire estate. He has no plans to retire today or even soon, but he does want to create a safety net by holding some capital independent of the business. He decides to create an ESOP and sell 30% of his interest. He now has a $3.6 million nest egg—and he still controls the business as majority shareholder. Also, he's one of the trustees of the ESOP, and as such, influences the voting power of the ESOP.

The ESOP borrows the $3.6 million from the bank to pay Walter for his shares, and then makes tax-deductible payments of $360,000 plus interest to the bank each year for 10 years. The transaction has cost the employees nothing. And when the loan is paid, they own 30% of the company. Walter, meanwhile, is nicely retired—his $3.6 million investment portfolio is doing nicely too, thank you—and he is *considering selling additional company shares to his ready-made market: the company's ESOP.*

Example 2

Stan and Ollie (okay, so these aren't their real names) are partners. Stan, who has no children, has sailboat brochures strewn across his desk. Retirement is in sight, and he's ready. Ollie's daughter is a V.P. of the company, and she's ready, too—for "Uncle Stan's" corner office.

But now Stan is starting to have second thoughts. If he sells his half of the business outright—a $3 million interest—he's looking at a capital gains tax bill of about a half-million dollars, plus the loss of his company car, his company-paid health plan, and so on. Can he, in fact, afford to retire?

And he's not hesitating alone. Ollie knows that in order to get Stan his $3 million, he—Ollie—must bring in $4.5 million before taxes. "Here's another fine mess you've gotten me into," says Ollie.

But Ollie's daughter really wants that office. She points out that if Stan creates an ESOP and sells his shares, he gets the full amount in cash to invest in qualified American securities. "And, Dad," she continues, "with the ESOP, it'll cost the company perhaps only $2 million to buy out Uncle Stan!"

"Brilliant," replies Ollie. "I'm glad I thought of it."

For the proper candidate, an ESOP can be a valuable planning tool, providing benefits for:

- *owners/shareholders,* who can cash out all or part of their corporate stock on a tax-deferred basis;
- *the corporation,* which can improve its debt-carrying capacity and cash flow; and
- *employees,* who have an opportunity to participate in and benefit from ownership of the company.

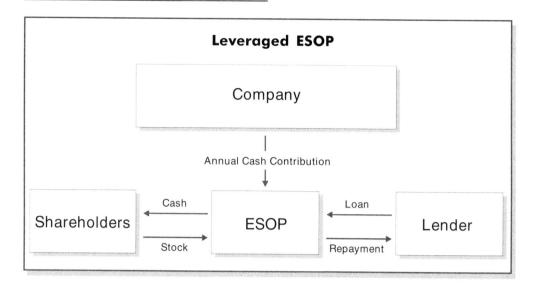

Leveraged ESOP

Company

Annual Cash Contribution

| Shareholders | Cash ← | ESOP | Loan ← | Lender |

Stock →

Repayment →

Chapter Summary

- An *employee stock ownership plan* (or "ESOP") is a qualified employer plan. It works much like a standard profit sharing plan, except that contributions are invested back into the company. Some of the reasons for using an ESOP are to increase employee loyalty, commitment, and productivity.

- Owners of a private company may initiate an ESOP in order to:
  - solve succession issues;
  - diversify personal net worth while retaining control;
  - recover previously paid corporate income taxes;
  - acquire another business with pre-tax dollars; or
  - convert from an existing plan.

- While it would seem that distributing stock to employees dilutes the owner's control over the company, such control continues to be maintained by strategically selecting the ESOP's trustees and by redeeming stock from retiring employees.

- An ESOP can be a valuable planning tool that provides benefits for:
  - owners/shareholders;
  - the corporation; and
  - employees.

10

Gifting the Business

"You can't escape the possibility of tomorrow
by evading it today."

—Abraham Lincoln

We have previously designated gifting as one of four owner exit strategies. In this chapter we'll delve deeper, exploring the ramifications of timing,
taxes, and specialized techniques.

To begin with, there are numerous ways to structure your gift:

- Gift the business and pay any applicable gift taxes. (Remember, an
  appraisal must be properly performed).
- Sell the business to your children at a modest price that would be
  acceptable to the IRS, but lower than that of going public or what
  a strategic buyer would pay. (A strategic buyer is someone who
  will pay more for a business than its fair market value because of
  the economies of scale achieved by buying the company.)
- Gift the business to a *family limited partnership* (FLP) or a *limited
  liability company* (LLC). (The business cannot be an "S" corporation.)
- Set up a *grantor-retained annuity trust* (GRAT), a *private annuity*, or
  a *defective grantor trust*.
- Use a *self-canceling installment note* (SCIN).

That's a lot of ways to give away slices of my own personal pie.
Back up, take it one step at a time, and convince me.

Understand, first of all, that's it's always better to do your gifting now. With the original asset taken out of your estate, it can grow and grow, with all appreciation intact, traveling tax-free down the roads you intend. If, on the other hand, you hold on to the asset and bequeath it at death, all that appreciation is subject to various taxes, which are payable by your beneficiaries.

But don't I have to pay gift taxes at the time of gifting, and don't gift taxes and estate taxes net the same result?

Probably so, and definitely not, in that order. And it's critical that you understand why.

You may have to pay a gift tax at the time of gifting, depending upon the size of the gift relative to your annual and lifetime allowances. But while gift and estate tax *rates* may be the same, it's cheaper by far to pay a gift tax now than an estate tax later. As a matter of fact:

$100 gifted *during life* costs $155,

but

$100 gifted *after death* costs $222!

How in the world do you figure that?

Quite simply, really. The gift tax is *tax exclusive*: it's imposed on the gift amount only, and only once. When property is transferred at death, there's an estate tax on the total bequest attributable to the property: it's *tax inclusive*.

Here's an example, assuming 55% estate and gift tax rates:

> *Joe wants his children to have $1 million in company stock. He signs it over to them, and pays a gift tax of $550,000—55% levied on top of the $1 million. He's therefore spent $1.55 million to gift $1 million. Joe is allowed to pay the gift tax, and that payment is not considered a taxable gift to the children.*

> *Pete, too, wants his children to have $1 million in company stock ...but not until after he dies. To do so, Pete's estate must designate $2.2 million for the gift. Only after the 55% estate tax—or $1.2 mil-*

> *lion—is* taken off *the $2.2 million, do the children
> get the intended $1 million.*

As you can see, paying a gift tax now is better than paying an estate tax later, not to mention the personal benefit of seeing your gift appreciated—and *appreciating*—during your lifetime. Of course, not everyone has the capital to make such a gift and pay the taxman now, so careful planning is the first order of good business.

What's the best way to gift assets?

As you might suspect, there is no "best way"…only the most advantageous way for *you*. Here are a number of proven—and surprisingly uncomplicated—techniques.

Family Limited Partnership

Let's consider Joe, from the previous example, who wants to give his children $1 million in company stock. Joe puts the stock into an FLP. Because the stock transfer is still considered a gift, there are gift taxes to pay. But first, two significant discounts are taken, resulting in a reduction of perhaps 20 to 40% of the original amount.

Why?

The government recognizes that limited partners cannot readily sell their shares, so there is no marketability.

Why not?

Because no one would buy them. They're not publicly traded, for one thing. For another, limited partners have no guaranteed rights to income. Interest can't be transferred without the permission of the general partner, and capital can't be withdrawn until the partnership ends.

Therefore, the general partner can take a discount. In addition, it's also assumed that limited partners with minority interest exercise little or no rights in the functioning of the company, so a second discount can be taken.

Even if no discounts were permitted, an FLP is still valuable—the parents still control the assets and distribution of income. Also, the existence of multiple partners can create certain income tax advantages.

An FLP can transfer business assets to the next generation, removing future growth from the estate (thus reducing estate taxes) while allowing the parent/owner to retain control of the business.

To summarize:

- The parents become *general partners*.
  - General partners can retain as little as 1% of the equity, but up to 100% of the vote and control.
  - General partners can receive an income stream from the business.
- The children become *limited partners*.
  - Limited partners receive the remainder of the equity, but only a minority (if any) vote.
  - Limited partners receive the benefit of the future appreciation of the business on an estate tax-free basis.
  - Income can be split among the general partner's children, which reduces income taxes.
- The value of the assets given to the limited partners is calculated on a discounted basis (due to the lack of marketability and control by the limited partners), further reducing any taxes due.
  - The discount typically ranges from 20 to 40%. (An independent valuation is needed.)
  - Although the valuation can be challenged, redirection of the discount to zero is unlikely.
- Because the assets have been gifted rather than transferred through the estate, the only tax due on the assets will be any applicable gift tax.
  - The $650,000 lifetime exemption (rising to $1 million) and $10,000 per person annual gift tax exemption can be used to shelter transferred assets from gift taxes.

Wait a minute—if I give my children 51% of the company stock, can't they control it, or even vote me out?

The limited partnership agreement is generally drafted to ensure against just that possibility. In fact, the FLP must, by law, be structured differently than a corporation with a board of directors. Thus, the general partner is pretty much just that—the company "general."

You might be interested in knowing that when Sam Walton died in 1993, he only owned 20% of the FLP he'd formed 40 years earlier.

Getting back to *our* owner—Joe—the $1 million gift has been reduced to $600,000 for tax purposes (assuming a 40% discount). The gift tax, then, is $330,000 instead of $550,000 (using a 55% gift tax rate for ease of illustration).

Joe has not only accomplished his goal of giving $1 million in stock to his children during his lifetime, but he's also saved $220,000 in current estate taxes. But more importantly, by using this very effective technique, Joe has removed a significant portion of the asset out of his personal estate, potentially saving over $2.3 million in future estate taxes (see the chart below). And, he does all this while retaining control over the *entire* asset.

Family Limited Partnership			
Comparison of taxes due on the transfer of an asseet worth $2,000,000: no planning versus the use of a family limited partnership			
	With No Planning	With a Family Limited Partnership	
	(Retain asset in estate)	General Partner Share (10%)	Limited Partner Share (90%)
Current value	$2,000,000	$200,000	$1,800,000
Future value[1]	$6,000,000	$600,000	$5,400,000
Estate tax[2]	$3,300,000	$330,000	N/A
Gift tax[3]	$0	$594,000	N/A
Total taxes	$3,300,000	$924,000	N/A
Tax savings	**$0**	**$2,376,000**	

[1] Assumed growth of asset over next 20 years.
[2] Assumes estate tax of 55% over entire projected future estate value (or general partner's share).
[3] Assumes a discount of 40% on the current gift (from $1,800,000 to $1,080,000) due to minority interest, and that the entire discounted amount of the gift is taxable (that is, it cannot be offset by the lifetime exemption).

Limited Liability Company

A gift may be made into a somewhat similar entity, the *limited liability company*. Offering many of the same benefits as an FLP, the LLC extends protection from personal liability to all its members. Complex structural differences between LLCs, FLPs, "C" corporations, and "S" corporations make legal and tax consultations of vital importance.

Grantor-Retained Annuity Trust (GRAT)

Under the terms of a GRAT, you place an income-producing asset in trust and you receive income from it over a period of your choosing. At the end of the period, the trust's beneficiaries assume ownership of its assets. The fair market value of the property, less the annuity, is considered a taxable gift.

While you cannot use your annual gift exclusion with a GRAT, you can credit your lifetime exemption to offset the gift. In theory—and in practice—by increasing the yearly annuity payment, the taxable gift can be effectively eliminated. This allows property to be transferred with virtually no gift tax cost.

The following chart shows annual payout amounts from a $1 million GRAT based on the age of the grantor and the term of the trust. Payment of these annual amounts will result in no material gift tax on the GRAT transfer.

GRAT Annual Payout			
Term of Trust*	Age 50	Age 60	Age 70
10 years	$146,464	$152,355	$165,511
15 years	114,981	122,215	138,737
20 years	100,833	109,579	129,518

Assumes $1,000,000 at 7% AFR (Applicable Federal Rate)

So, for $1 million held in trust, a 50-year-old would receive $114,981 a year for 15 years. There is no gift tax on the transfer, and no estate tax after 15 years. And, assuming the asset grows to $3 million over the 15 years, the estate tax savings would be $1,650,000.

You can probably guess my next question: what's the downside?

The underlying variable is whether the trust survives you, or you survive the trust. If you outlive the trust, all goes as planned: the income you receive each year discounts the value of the gift, which passes out of your estate and on to your beneficiaries. However, if you die before the end of the trust period, the GRAT's assets revert to your estate and are subject to the full spectrum of taxes due.

So how do you "hedge your bet"? The GRAT's heirs should consider funding an irrevocable life insurance trust to cover potential taxes. Choose a term policy for the life of the trust, or a permanent policy to achieve specific and personal goals and objectives.

Private Annuity

A private annuity is a vehicle that you should consider if you're looking for steady income. It's particularly advantageous when an early death occurs.

Here's how it works. An asset capable of producing income is transferred by a transferor (the annuitant), thereby removing it from the estate. In return, the transferee (the payor) makes regular payments to the transferor for a specified period—usually the lifetime of the transferor and/or the transferor's spouse—using income from the transferred asset.

The private annuity is a useful tool for an individual who wants to spread the gain from a highly appreciated asset over his or her life expectancy. It is also a useful estate tax saving tool because, by design, payments end when the transferor dies and the entire value of the asset is immediately removed from the estate.

For example, a couple with a 20-year joint life expectancy transfers an asset with a fair market value of $1 million, and they receive annuity payments of approximately $111,000 a year from the payor. Depending on the couple's basis in the asset, some of the $111,000 is considered tax-free (return of principal), some is subject to capital gains tax, and some to regular income tax. If the couple were to pass away during the fifth year, the annuity ends, the payor owns the asset, and there is no estate tax on the original $1 million. Whenever the couple dies, the transfer is deemed completed.

The ideal transferor-payor situation is one that meets the following criteria:

- The transferor is in a high estate tax bracket or has no marital deduction.
- The property is capable of producing at least some income and/or is appreciating rapidly.
- The payor is capable of paying the promised amounts (at least in part).

- The parties trust each other (because the private annuity is unsecured).

- The transferor has other assets and sources of income.

- The transferor has a less-than-average life expectancy (which makes the arrangement a "bargain" for the payor).

What disadvantages should I consider?

There are risks involved with a private annuity. Before you decide to use one, be sure to consider the following points:

- The asset may not appreciate or produce sufficient income to make the annuity payments.

- Significant interest rate increases can result in below-market payments.

- If the transferor outlives his or her life expectancy, the payor's liability can be greater than projected.

- The payor cannot deduct any portion of the payments as a business expense.

What about gift taxes?

There are none. The private annuity is considered a private transaction—a simple exchange of one asset for another.

Self-Canceling Installment Note

A SCIN (pronounced like "skin") is typically used to sell a business or other property to children or grandchildren with minimal gift and estate tax consequences. Usually, you can set the sale price somewhat lower than you would if you were selling to an outside party, but be aware that an unreasonably low price tends to attract the attention of the IRS.

Here's how it works: the purchasers pay an agreed-upon amount for an agreed-upon period. If the seller dies before the period is up, the balance is nullified, ending the buyer's obligation to pay, and the balance remains outside the estate.

Wait a minute—shouldn't the unpaid balance of the fair market value be included in the estate?

That's how it generally works, yes—but not if you use a properly designed SCIN.

How is a SCIN properly designed?

There are three important obligations to be met:

1. The cancellation provision must be "bargained for" as part of the consideration for the sale.
2. The purchase price must reflect this bargain, either with a principal risk premium (above market sales price) or an interest rate premium (above market interest rate).
3. The seller may not retain any control after the sale.

And what if it's **not** properly designed?

The seller may be deemed to have made a part-sale, part-gift. If any of the remaining interest (the canceled payments) is considered a gift, the entire value of the property, less the consideration actually paid, will be included in the decedent's gross estate.

How do I decide whether to reflect the risk premium as an increase in the sales price or as an increase in the interest rate?

That depends on the relative tax situations of the buyer and the seller. If the risk premium is reflected in the sales price (principal risk premium), the seller will report more of each payment as capital gain and less as interest income. The buyer will pay less interest (which is deductible if the interest is trade or business interest and not personal interest), but his or her basis will be higher. If the property is depreciable and the buyer and seller are in similar tax brackets, the principal risk premium may be preferred to give the buyer a larger depreciable base.

However, if the property is not depreciable, the buyer may prefer the interest rate premium where the basis is lower but deductible interest payments are higher.

Either way, the same $1 million private annuity sale that resulted in annual payments of $111,000 could result in payments of $127,000 with a SCIN. That's the impact of the risk premium.

Is there a down side to using a SCIN?

There are disadvantages—or more precisely, *considerations*—to bear in mind:

- The premium represents a higher price, whether included in the principal or the interest rate.
- Subsequent sales by family members cannot be prevented.
- There is a risk of interest rate fluctuation.

Please note that there are other tax consequences inherent with both the SCIN and the private annuity. Your accountant or attorney can explain these in detail.

Defective Grantor Trust

In a defective grantor trust, the assets are sold via an installment note to an irrevocable trust established by the grantor. The note is structured so that the trust pays the interest only, with a balloon payment later. It can also be structured to receive principal payments, if desired. The trust itself is written so as to intentionally violate one of the grantor trust rules, causing the income of the trust to be taxed to the grantor rather than to the trust. The tax paid by the grantor is not considered a gift to the beneficiaries.

Defective? *I don't think I like the sound of that.*

You'll like the tax benefits, through.

Although designing the trust requires intricate planning, I'll try to keep the explanation simple. The table on the next page breaks the process down, step by step.

Can you give me an example?

Sure. Let's say that you sell your business to a defective grantor trust for $10 million, with the note owed, of course, to you. Three years later, the business is sold to a third party for $15 million. The trust pays off the note, and the excess $5 million is shifted to your children, free of estate taxes. In the years before the trust asset is sold, you—the grantor—pay the income tax on net earnings.

Defective Grantor Trust

- The seller-grantor creates a defective grantor trust with a substantial "seed money" gift.

- The grantor sells the property (reflecting appropriate valuation discounts) to the defective grantor trust in return for a bona fide promissory note. (Property can be closely-held stock [including S corp stock], publicly traded stock, partnership interests, real estate, etc.). Because the trust is a grantor trust for income tax purposes, the current IRS position is that no capital gain is recognized from the sale and the seller's basis carries over to the trust.

- The promissory note pays interest only at the IRS Applicable Federal Rate (AFR) during the note term, typically with a balloon principal payment due at the end of the term.

- The transaction takes place with no income tax, gift tax (on the seed money gift), or generation-skipping transfer (GST) tax (assuming there is sufficient GST exemptions to exempt the seed money gift). The result is maximum tax "leverage."

- At death, only the note value plus the accumulated interest should be included in the seller's estae, and all post-sale property appreciation should be immediately excludable from the estate. In addition, the seller's payment of income taxes on the grantor trust income (without reimbursement) further reduces his or her estate.

- The defective grantor trust can purchase life insurance on the seller's life. The life insurance can be set up on a split-dollar basis, if desired.

- The defective grantor trust applies the insurance proceeds to repay its note at the seller's death (without having to sell low-basis trust assets), and to purchase other estate assets or make loans to the estate.

- The estate can use the cash received from the defective grantor trust to pay estate taxes and fund other liquidity needs.

What about the capital gains tax?

This tax is also paid by the grantor, which is another advantage to the children.

A defective grantor trust can be a very useful tool in the right circumstances. Be sure to consult qualified legal and/or tax advisors on the use of all of these techniques.

Chapter Summary

- One of four possible owner exit strategies is gifting a business. Ways to structure the gift include:
  - gifting the company and paying applicable taxes;
  - selling to your children;
  - gifting to a *family limited partnership*;
  - forming a *limited liability company*;
  - setting up a *grantor retained annuity trust*, a *private annuity*, or a *self-canceling installment note*; and
  - using a *defective grantor trust*.

- It's always better to do gifting now, thus taking the original asset out of your estate. A gift tax paid now is considerably less expensive than paying an estate tax later because:
  - a gift tax is *tax exclusive*; and
  - an estate tax is *tax inclusive*.

Part Two:

ESTATE PLANNING

11

Estate Planning Overview

*"There is nothing sinister in so arranging one's
affairs as to keep taxes as low as possible. Every-
body does so, rich or poor; and all do right, for
nobody owes any public duty to pay more than the
law demands; taxes are enforced extractions, not
voluntary contributions."*

—Judge Learned Hand

And now, let's shift gears.

Why?

It's time we talked about your *personal* assets. Personal estate planning is a logical and necessary extension of business succession planning. Like succession planning, estate planning allows you to transfer wealth to your designated beneficiaries in a logical, orderly, tax-advantaged way. Unfortunately, though, there is one aspect of estate planning that can be a problem.

What's that?

The fact that most people aren't overly eager to tackle it. Estate planning is all too easy to put off. Maybe you think it's too early, or that your estate is too small.

But don't make that mistake. When you've spent so many years building your estate, shouldn't you be willing to spend more than just a few hours figuring out how to pass it to your family?

The chart on the next page brings the issue home.

Six Reasons to Plan Your Estate	
Without an Estate Plan:	**With an Estate Plan:**
1. State laws determine who inherits your assets—they could pass to an estranged relative.	You decide who receives your assets.
2. The terms and timing of the distribution of your assets are set by law. Your children could be left in unfettered control of a sizable estate.	You decide how and when your beneficiaries will receive their inheritance.
3. The court appoints administrators for your estate—whose ideas may not be compatible with your own.	You decide who will manage your estate (executor, trustees, etc.).
4. Settlement costs are usually greater without an estate plan, due to required administrative expenses and unnecessary taxes.	You can reduce estate taxes and administrative expenses.
5. The court appoints a guardian for your minor child(ren).	You select a guardian for your child(ren).
6. Financial loss and family hardships may result from an untimely forced sale of a family business.	You can provide for the orderly continuance or sale of a family business.

There are, tragically, too many famous examples of estates lost or devastated due to lack of proper planning. The graphic on the next page illustrates this point well.

Wow! You mean one of the most famous of all accountants lost over half his estate to taxes and other costs?

You mean his *heirs* lost. And they're hardly alone. Here are some traps into which even the richest of the rich—and smartest of the smart—have fallen:

Five Common Mistakes Made by Wealthy Individuals and Business Owners

1. Losing 50% or more of your net worth to taxes.
2. Failing to leverage your IRA, pension, profit sharing, or 401(k) plan.
3. Thinking liquidity will solve your estate tax problems.
4. Failing to utilize charitable bequests, annual gifts, and lifetime exemptions to significantly reduce estate and income taxes.
5. Failing to set up a business succession plan.

Sample Estate Distribution

Alwin C. Ernst
Founder of Ernst & Ernst, Certified Public Accountants

Gross estate	**$12,642,431**
Federal estate tax	$5,812,281
California estate tax	$1,226,737
Administrative fees	$ 58,862
Executor's fees	$ 10,000
Attorney's fees	$ 10,000
Debt	$ 6,232
Total costs	$ 7,124,112
Net estate	**$ 5,518,319**

Net Estate: 44%   Taxes & Fees: 56%

SHRINKAGE: 56%

Well, I don't claim to be among the richest of the rich or the smartest of the smart, but it sounds like I can avoid the same trap into which they fell.

No doubt about it. By starting now, you can recover the ball you fumbled on the goal line, and develop some new plays to get into the end zone pretty much untouched. The first thing you want to do is organize and implement a wealth transfer strategy.

What do you mean by wealth "transfer"?

A strategic wealth transfer is the orderly *shifting* of goods, property, and resources currently in your name—in the most tax-efficient way, while you're living—to another person or entity that you designate. This is the first of five estate planning goals that are easily achievable now, but a lot harder (if not impossible) when you're gone.

Goals of Proper Estate Planning

- Maximize wealth transfer.
- Distribute assets equitably to beneficiaries and/or charities in a manner consistent with your values.
- Determine control while living.
- Designate control after death.
- Minimize taxation.

How do I start?

Do two things: first, determine *who* gets *what* and *when*; second, decide how much reduction of your estate, due to estate taxes, you will accept.

And then what?

Chart your game plan. Establish strategies for distributing your assets, reducing tax liability, and paying taxes. There are techniques and tools that can help you to accomplish your life's goals.

You may be tempted to fall into the conventional planning trap of simply accepting the amount of taxes the government will take out of your estate. It would certainly be easier to shrug the whole thing off as a problem your children will have to deal with when you're gone, but that's not an efficient approach. Sophisticated planning is a proactive *process*, not simply an event, which minimizes taxes and maximizes distribution of your estate to beneficiaries and charities. In fact, estate taxes can be completely eliminated with proper planning, but they tend to compound themselves when there is little or no planning.

In the next several chapters, we'll explore ways to ensure that your heirs not only don't *lose*…but, indeed, have a lot to *gain*.

Chapter Summary

- Estate planning is easy to put off, either because people think it's too early or because they believe that their estate is too small to warrant planning.

- Five common mistakes made by wealthy individuals and business owners include:

  - losing half or more of net worth to taxes;

  - failing to leverage IRA, pension, profit sharing, or 401(k) plans;

  - thinking that liquidity will solve estate tax problems;

  - failing to utilize charitable bequests, annual gifts, and lifetime exemptions to reduce taxes; and

  - failing to set up a business succession plan.

- Five goals of proper estate planning include:

  - maximizing wealth transfer;

  - distributing assets equitably to beneficiaries and/or charities in a manner consistent with your values;

  - determining control while living;

  - designating control after death; and

  - minimizing taxation.

- Efficient estate planning involves (1) developing a *wealth transfer strategy*, and (2) establishing a plan to achieve it. A good plan consists of strategies to efficiently facilitate asset distribution, tax reduction, and tax payment.

- Estate taxes can be significantly reduced or eliminated with proper planning.

- Sophisticated estate planning is an outstanding investment for your family.

12

Estate Taxes

"It has been estimated that more than ten trillion
dollars of assets will be transferred in the next few
decades, with staggering estate tax consequences."

—USA Today
January 8, 1999

I know that tax laws change constantly. But please, before we go
on, clear up a basic question: how much will my spouse get free and
clear?

Providing he or she is a U.S. citizen, we can answer that in one word:
everything.

The Economic Recovery Act of 1981 allows for an "unlimited marital
deduction," which takes effect in one of three ways:

1. Any bequests you make to your spouse pass from your estate to
   your spouse's, free from estate taxes.
2. All joint property automatically goes to your spouse.
3. You may create a marital trust, with all assets controlled by your
   surviving spouse.

So if I die I can leave my wife everything, and she pays no estate
taxes.

Right. But that may not be the best way to accomplish your *long-term* goal
of leaving your family or favorite charities as much as possible (and the
taxman as little as possible).

Unified Transfer Tax Schedule

Amount of Transfer	Rate of Tax
Not over $10,000	18% of such amount
Over $10,000 but not over $20,000	$1,800 plus 20% of excess over $10,000
Over $20,000 but not over $40,000	$3,800 plus 22% of excess over $20,000
Over $40,000 but not over $60,000	$8,200 plus 24% of excess over $40,000
Over $60,000 but not over $80,000	$13,000 plus 26% of excess over $60,000
Over $80,000 but not over $100,000	$18,000 plus 28% of excess over $80,000
Over $100,000 but not over $150,000	$23,800 plus 30% of excess over $100,000
Over $150,000 but not over $250,000	$38,000 plus 32% of excess over $150,000
Over $250,000 but not over $500,000	$70,800 plus 34% of excess over $250,000
Over $500,000 but not over $750,000	$155,800 plus 37% of excess over $500,000
Over $750,000 but not over $1,000,000	$248,300 plus 39% of excess over $750,000
Over $1,000,000 but not over $1,250,000	$345,800 plus 41% of excess over $1,000,000
Over $1,250,000 but not over $1,500,000	$448,300 plus 43% of excess over $1,250,000
Over $1,500,000 but not over $2,000,000	$555,800 plus 45% of excess over $1,500,000
Over $2,000,000 but not over $2,500,000	$780,800 plus 49% of excess over $2,000,000
Over $2,500,000 but not over $3,000,000	$1,025,800 plus 53% of excess over $2,500,000
Over $3,000,000	$1,290,800 plus 55% of excess over $3,000,000*

*The 1987 tax code added a 5% excise tax penalty on transferred amounts between $10 million and $21 million. The effect is to phase out the benefit of the tax credit on the exemption equivalent, as well as the benefit of the graduated rates on the first $3 million of transferred assets. The upper end of this bracket is increasing as a result of the Taxpayer Relief Act of 1997, from $21,040,000 in 1997 to $24,100,000 in 2006 and thereafter. Once the total exceeds the upper end of this bracket, the estate tax is a flat 55% of the entire estate.

Unified Credit and Exemption Equivalent

Year	Unified Credit*	Exemption Equivalent*
1997	$192,800	$600,000
1998	$202,500	$625,000
1999	$211,300	$650,000
2000-01	$220,550	$675,000
2002-03	$229,800	$700,000
2004	$287,300	$850,000
2005	$326,300	$950,000
2006 and beyond	$345,800	$1,000,000

*The Taxpayer Relief Act of 1997 refers to the unified credit as the "applicable credit amount," and to the exemption equivalent as the "applicable exclusion amount."

How do I do that?

By using the "unified credit." This is an amount that may be passed from your estate to someone *other* than your spouse on a tax-free basis. Children are most commonly the beneficiaries of this credit, but it's an amount that you may leave to *anyone*, during your lifetime or after death.

The unified credit may be one of the most important ideas I cover in this book—and one of the easiest to execute. Because it's so critical, I'll explain it slowly and simply.

The slow and simple among us thank you in advance.

Let's begin with some background. Created under the 1976 Tax Reform Act, the unified credit granted taxpayers a credit of up to $192,800 against taxes stemming from cumulative dispositions of property. That credit was equivalent to the taxes on $600,000 of property, which is therefore referred to as the "exemption equivalent."

Stop right there. I thought the estate tax was 55%. Even the slow and simple can see that $192,800 is less than 55% of $600,000.

Exactly right. The chart on the previous page (which also was created by the Tax Reform Act) shows the graduated rates created for both estate and gift taxes, which range from 18% to 55%.

As you can see, $600,000 falls within the 37% rate of taxation. The 55% bracket, in fact, doesn't kick in until you reach $3 million in estate property transfers.

Now, before we go any further, let's get that $600,000 figure out of your head because it became obsolete with The Taxpayer Relief Act of 1997. The unified credit and the exemption equivalent were increased according to the table opposite.

Then beginning in the year 2006, I'll be able to leave a million dollars to anyone I want before and/or after I die, and there won't be any estate taxes due?

Correct. And remember, this "lifetime exclusion" doesn't have to be cash. It's basically anything of measurable value out of your gross estate, including all of your solely owned property.

Another important thing to remember: these exclusions are *per individual*, so all of the figures shown thus far in this chapter *double* for a married couple.

So my wife and I together can leave $2 million, estate tax-free, if we die after 2006?

Yes…which brings up the critical point of why leaving all your solely owned assets to your spouse is *not* the best way to go.

*I think I'm ahead of you for once. If I leave her everything, and she can eventually only leave her **own** exemption equivalent, we lose **my** exemption equivalent because it became part of her estate.*

Perfectly put. "Use it or lose it" should be the rallying cry of all those whose estates will be subject to taxes. The exemption equivalent is the easiest way to instantly reduce your gross estate for tax purposes, which can benefit your heirs by hundreds of thousands of dollars…or more.

*Or **more**? What am I missing?*

It's not what you're missing, but what your heirs may be *gaining* by the wise use of the exemption equivalent. Remember, you're not just leaving them the exemption amount—which is $650,000 for 1999—but what it becomes *after* it's removed from your estate. All appreciation will grow out of the estate also, and thus estate tax-free. (Of course, I'm *only* referring to estate taxes here; income and/or capital gains taxes may be applicable as the asset appreciates.) A transfer of stock in your own family business, for example, can now be applied toward the lifetime exclusion. Assuming that the stock will be worth more at the time of your death, taking those shares out of your estate today could result in significant tax savings down the road.

What if I want to exclude the allowable amount from my estate, but I don't want to surrender control of the assets right now?

There are a variety of instruments designed for just such a purpose. For instance, you could use a family limited partnership, where you are the general partner owning a small percentage of the partnership. Alternatively, you could form a limited liability company where you are the managing member owning a small percentage of the corporation. Or, you could issue two classes of stock: voting and non-voting. I'll discuss all of these techniques in more detail later.

Chapter Summary

- The Economic Recovery Act of 1981 permits an "unlimited marital deduction," which takes effect in one of the following ways:
  - Any bequests made to a spouse are free from estate taxes.
  - All joint property automatically passes to the spouse.
  - A marital trust may be created, with all assets controlled by the surviving spouse.

- The "unified credit" grants taxpayers a credit against taxes stemming from cumulative distributions of property. The amount of property exempted is called the "exemption equivalent," and may be distributed during and/or after the owner's lifetime.

- The Taxpayer Relief Act of 1997 created a new table of exemption equivalents, which increase to $1,000,000 in the year 2006. In addition to cash, this exemption may consist of any solely owned property with measurable value. All amounts double for a married couple.

- Leaving solely owned assets to a surviving spouse may not be good planning, as the decedent's personal exemption equivalent—and its potential appreciation in value outside of the estate—is lost.

- There are a variety of instruments designed to remove property from an estate without surrendering control over it, including family limited partnerships, limited liability companies, and voting/non-voting stock arrangements.

13

Wills and Trusts

"Not to decide is to decide."

—Harvey Cox
American Theologian and Author

Imagine, if you will, a typical scene from an Agatha Christie-style mystery:

> *A wealthy patriarch has died, and a group of people is gathered around the ornate drawing room table in his dark, drafty old mansion. At the head of the table is another elderly person—a lawyer or banker—who is solemnly reading the deceased's last will and testament. Lightning crashes intermittently from the terrible storm raging outside, briefly illuminating the greedy faces of the old gentleman's relatives. Before the night is over, one or more of those in the room will join the dear departed, a victim of familial avarice and malevolence.*

This is a bit dramatic, isn't it?

Perhaps. But you can believe that it's going to get pretty dramatic around *someone's* table if most of your estate is liquidated to pay taxes. So let's talk about wills.

But first, let's talk about a lack of wills, which is legally known as "intestacy."

A will is a legal document that controls the distribution of your assets after your death. If you do not prepare a will, you die intestate, leaving no distribution plan for your assets.

What happens then?

In such a case, distribution will be determined by the intestacy laws of the state you live in. In general, if you have a spouse but no children, half of your estate would go to him or her, and half to your parents if they survive you. If you have children, half of your estate would go to your spouse, and the remaining half would be divided among your children. If the children were minors, distribution would be handled through probate court.

The question to ask yourself before going any further is:

Is this how I would want my estate to be distributed?

I'll assume the answer is "no." So, next question:

Do I want my heirs to go through the expense, delay, and public disclosure of probate?

I'm not even going to wait for your answer. Let's just move on.

Many people are able to get by with a simple will. To wit: "I leave everything to my wife." Such an instrument would also go through probate, so this is where "titling" is important to coordinate with the will. This will be covered in the next chapter.

With a simple will, however, you may miss out on opportunities to work within the system to avoid or minimize taxes.

The individual unified transfer tax credit, discussed in the previous chapter, is a perfect example of an opportunity that can become a costly *missed* opportunity if it isn't used properly.

I'll illustrate such a worst-case scenario:

> *Let's assume that you and your wife are 55 years old, and that you are presently maintaining owner-ship of a $1 million dollar asset. Let's also assume that it enjoys steady growth at a rate of 7% annu-*

ally. When you reach age 65, the asset will be worth approximately $2 million; at 75, it'll be worth $4 million; and when you're age 85 its value will have increased to $8 million. At age 85, both you and your wife pass away, leaving the asset in your estate.

The estate taxes that will be due on the now-$8 million asset will total approximately $4 million— all because you chose to leave the asset in your estate. As you can see, the future tax could be four times *the value of the original asset!*

Ouch! I can see why you call it a "worst case." Let's get to the good part.

Okay. If you and your wife don't need the asset and you gift it to your children *today* using the transfer tax credit exemption, you will save $4 million in estate taxes. Or more precisely, you'll save your *children* $4 million.

So when we talk about estate taxes, we're really talking about what the next generation pays, not my wife.

Exactly. You can leave your entire estate to your spouse—no matter what the amount—totally free from estate taxes thanks to the unlimited marital deduction. But again, you have the ability to take your unified credit amount out of your estate—before or after your death—and gift it free from taxes. *How* you gift it is what impacts the total tax benefit.

Do you mean putting the credit into a trust?

Yes. And while there are numerous names for such an instrument, the *A-B trust* seems to be the most useful. It's easy to remember, and describes the necessity for the creation of two separate trusts.

Why two trusts?

The *A trust* is also known as the marital trust. With the exception of the property constituting your lifetime exemption, your assets are transferred to your spouse upon your death, estate tax-free, through the unlimited marital deduction. Your surviving spouse controls the A trust and has complete access to both its principal and income.

*And the **B trust** is the exemption property?*

Right. It's known alternatively as the "credit shelter trust," "exemption trust," or "bypass trust" because it's intended for beneficiaries other than the spouse, and it consists of assets with a value equal to the lifetime exemption

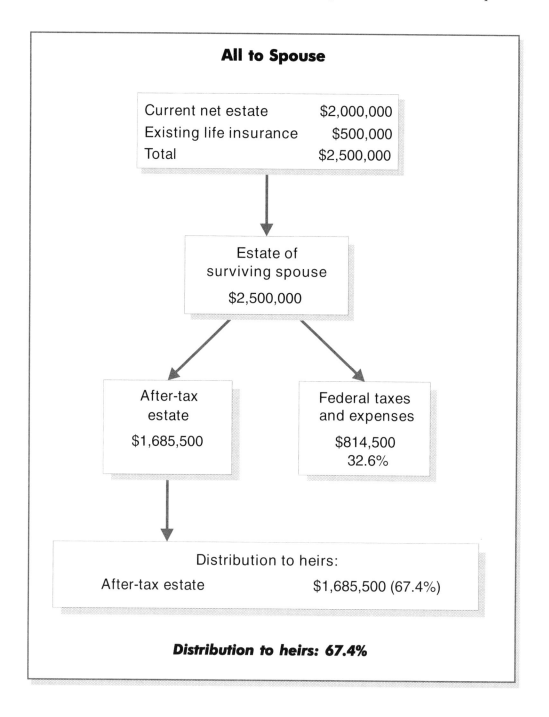

All to Spouse

Current net estate	$2,000,000
Existing life insurance	$500,000
Total	$2,500,000

Estate of
surviving spouse
$2,500,000

After-tax
estate
$1,685,500

Federal taxes
and expenses
$814,500
32.6%

Distribution to heirs:
After-tax estate $1,685,500 (67.4%)

Distribution to heirs: 67.4%

(therefore bypassing estate taxes). The trustee can pay income from the trust to your spouse and/or your children. Significantly, all appreciation within the trust occurs outside either spouse's estate, which makes the trust a great place for investments that are likely to enjoy significant growth.

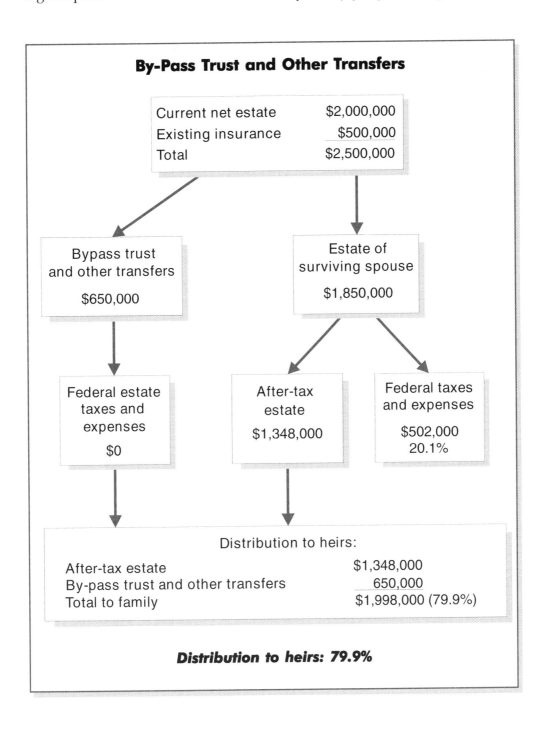

By-Pass Trust and Other Transfers

Current net estate	$2,000,000
Existing insurance	$500,000
Total	$2,500,000

Bypass trust and other transfers

$650,000

Estate of surviving spouse

$1,850,000

Federal estate taxes and expenses

$0

After-tax estate

$1,348,000

Federal taxes and expenses

$502,000
20.1%

Distribution to heirs:

After-tax estate	$1,348,000
By-pass trust and other transfers	650,000
Total to family	$1,998,000 (79.9%)

Distribution to heirs: 79.9%

You can establish it by using one of two vehicles: a living trust or a testamentary trust. The difference between a living trust and a testamentary trust is the point in time at which assets are distributed. A testamentary trust is funded at death, through your will, while a living trust is established during your lifetime.

Is there an advantage to one over the other?

The advantage of the living trust is that it avoids probate. You can, in effect, be your own trustee. You keep your financial affairs private, and you save the cost and delay of the probate process.

Tell me, what do most people do?

One of the most popular strategies used by sophisticated estate planners today is a *pour-over will with a living revocable trust.*

The will itself is a relatively brief document that basically says, "When I die, I'm leaving all of my assets to my trust." The trust is a "living" document, which means it allows you to avoid probate, and it's "revocable," which means you reserve the right to change, amend, or alter it after it's drafted.

How does a "revocable" trust differ from an "irrevocable" trust, apart from the obvious advantage of being able to change it later on?

That important feature comes with a price—it's taxable. Assets held in a revocable trust are included in your estate; assets in an irrevocable trust are not. Anything in your control is taxable; anything out of your control is not.

What am I giving up by avoiding taxes through an irrevocable trust?

As you mentioned, the ability to change it. Therefore, what's generally in an irrevocable trust is an insurance policy. You can't change the policy, but you *can* effectively cancel it by not gifting premiums to the trust. However, irrevocable trusts owning insurance can solve a multitude of problems. They can pay estate taxes, provide direct assets for children or other heirs, provide for children with special needs, provide liquidity for debt, and so on.

How an Insurance Trust Works

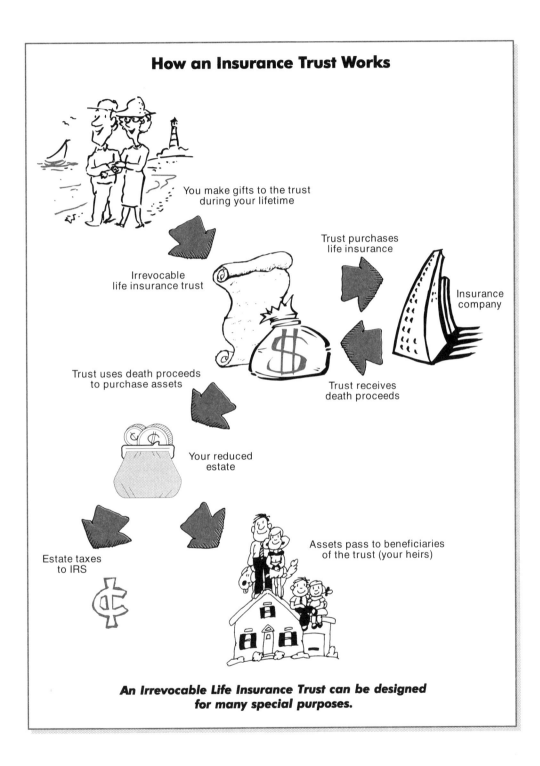

You make gifts to the trust
during your lifetime

Irrevocable
life insurance trust

Trust purchases
life insurance

Insurance
company

Trust uses death proceeds
to purchase assets

Trust receives
death proceeds

Your reduced
estate

Estate taxes
to IRS

Assets pass to beneficiaries
of the trust (your heirs)

***An Irrevocable Life Insurance Trust can be designed
for many special purposes.***

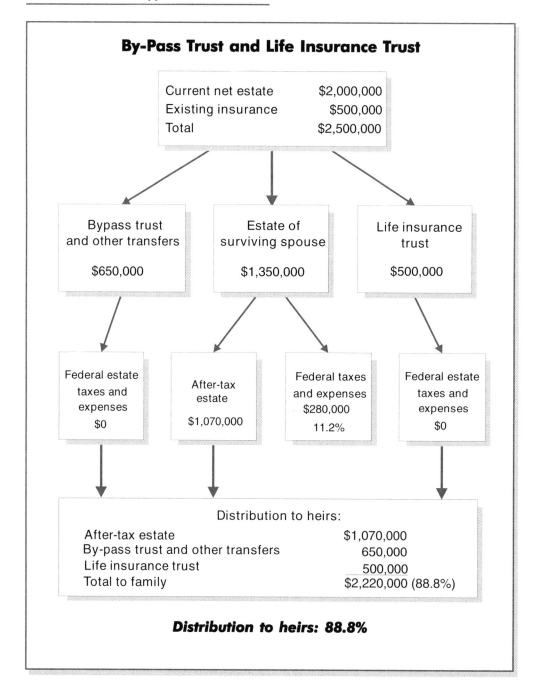

By-Pass Trust and Life Insurance Trust

Current net estate	$2,000,000
Existing insurance	$500,000
Total	$2,500,000

Bypass trust and other transfers

$650,000

Estate of surviving spouse

$1,350,000

Life insurance trust

$500,000

Federal estate taxes and expenses

$0

After-tax estate

$1,070,000

Federal taxes and expenses $280,000

11.2%

Federal estate taxes and expenses

$0

Distribution to heirs:

After-tax estate	$1,070,000
By-pass trust and other transfers	650,000
Life insurance trust	500,000
Total to family	$2,220,000 (88.8%)

Distribution to heirs: 88.8%

I see. Now, tell me about using a pour-over will with a living revocable trust.

This document is designed to address many financial issues. Some of these issues may seem trivial, but your attention to detail now enables you to determine the destiny of your estate far into the future. Have you thought about issues such as:

- Who will be your successor trustee?
- At what ages should your heirs receive their distributions?
- Should distributions to the children be in lump sums?
- Who will be your children's guardian, if such a decision becomes necessary?
- What decision-making powers will the guardian have?
- How much power should be left to the trustee in terms of managing your estate? Will the trustee be able to restrict distributions in the event of possible or actual misuse?
- Who would be the next (and/or contingent) successor trustee, and the next (and/or contingent) guardian?
- Who would be the alternative beneficiaries if a tragedy were to befall your children?
- How much flexibility should you grant to your surviving spouse? Should he or she:
  - have complete control over everything? (Remember, your surviving spouse could, for example, turn everything over to a new spouse.)
  - receive interest income only, with the principal payable at the trustee's discretion? (Perhaps your spouse could be granted an emergency right to withdraw a portion of the principal.)
- If you have children from more than one marriage, should a companion "QTIP trust" be created which pre-determines successive ownership according to your wishes?

A "QTIP trust?" What on earth is that?

In these days of multiple marriages, it is understandable that wealthy estate owners are concerned about the equitable distribution of their assets. A particular concern deals not with the first transfer of assets upon the death of the owner—to the spouse, using the unlimited marital deduction allowance—but with the dispersal of assets following the spouse's death.

Cathy is Tony's second wife. Tony is supporting one child from his first marriage, and Cathy has two children from her previous marriage. Tony wants to provide for Cathy upon his death, but when she dies, Tony wants to be sure that his assets pass to his natural child.

A *qualified terminable interest property* (or "QTIP") *trust* will satisfy Tony's wishes by eliminating Cathy's "power of appointment," which is her ability to determine the ultimate distribution of trust assets at her death.

By eliminating this power of appointment and utilizing a QTIP trust, Tony directs that Cathy will receive all annual income generated by a given asset—corporate stock, for example. However, the principal—the stock itself—goes to Tony's child upon Cathy's death. Cathy can't change that.

So, again…have you thought about such things?

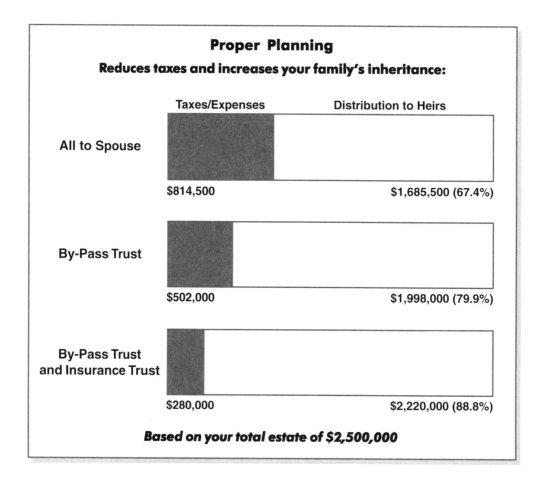

Proper Planning

Reduces taxes and increases your family's inheritance:

	Taxes/Expenses	Distribution to Heirs
All to Spouse	$814,500	$1,685,500 (67.4%)
By-Pass Trust	$502,000	$1,998,000 (79.9%)
By-Pass Trust and Insurance Trust	$280,000	$2,220,000 (88.8%)

Based on your total estate of $2,500,000

Are you kidding? I haven't even thought about what I'm going to have for lunch.

And therein lies the sad but common tale of business owners—and their advisors—who are so busy putting out the daily brush fires that they don't see the forest fire creeping up slowly but inevitably upon them. And what about your surviving spouse? Will he or she be as able as you are to discuss and decide upon such vital issues as these?

Planning now gives you a position of strength, *before* the decisions are forced upon you...and, frankly, before some of the available options are no longer available.

Chapter Summary

- A will is a legal document that controls the distribution of your assets after your death. If no will is prepared, your estate distributions are determined by state "intestacy" laws.
- Many people have a simple will. However, significant opportunities to avoid or minimize taxes may be missed if your estate plan stops there.
- An *A-B trust* can be a powerful tool.
  - The *A trust*, known as the marital trust, contains everything you wish to leave to your spouse *except* the property constituting your lifetime exemption.
  - The *B trust* contains assets with a value equal to the lifetime exemption for beneficiaries other than your spouse, and bypasses estate taxes. It's especially appropriate for investments that are likely to grow.
- An A-B trust can be established through a living trust (established during one's lifetime) or through a testamentary trust (funded at death). A living trust avoids probate.
- A *pour-over will with a living revocable trust* is a popular alternative, but there are advantages and disadvantages that should be considered carefully.
- Planning now gives you a position of strength. Planning later may make certain options unavailable.

14

Titling

"Put not your trust in money, but put your money in trust."

—Oliver Wendell Holmes, 1809-94
American Physician and Author

The thrust of this book thus far has been to provide you with an incentive to begin planning the rest of your life so as to benefit not only yourself, but also your spouse and heirs.

That said, the purpose of this chapter is to start you thinking about *un*-doing some things you may have already done that could negatively impact you, your spouse, and your children.

Which would be...

Titling. As you know, there must be a legal owner or owners for any asset, whether it's cash or land or stocks or collectibles. As we've discussed, the owner can be a person or an entity—a trust, for example.

You've spent your life accumulating things to own. And you take well-deserved pride in your ownership. Now, however, is the time to think whether you're best served by *not* owning those very things you worked so hard to acquire.

Now that I just don't get.

What I mean is, determining the type of ownership that will work best to preserve a given asset when it's passed to a new owner upon the death of the original owner.

Let's consider three types of ownership, and the tax consequences of each at death:

- **Individual ownership** allows a step-up in basis, but may be subject to probate.

- **Joint ownership** allows a step-up in basis for half of the property, and avoids probate.

- **Trust ownership** allows assets a step-up in basis and avoids probate *if* the trust is drafted properly and the asset is titled to the trust.

If assets are owned jointly with rights of survivorship, everything in the deceased's estate goes directly to the spouse. There are advantages to this arrangement: the transition is quick and automatic, and it avoids probate. But you *lose* advantages to which you and your spouse are legally entitled.

Such as the unified tax credit?

Yes…the very foundation on which so many other asset preservation techniques are based. If you don't use your lifetime exemption, either during life or upon your death, those otherwise exempted assets—and their appreciation—are passed into the survivor's estate and subject to all applicable taxes upon his or her subsequent death.

This is a good time to remind you that your spouse also has a unified tax credit exemption. But if he or she dies before you do without taking advantage of the tax credit, at least one of your two exemptions is automatically lost.

What about the limit of a 50% step-up in basis? How does that work?

If you paid $100,000 for a jointly-held stock that is now worth $1 million, your surviving spouse, *upon selling the stock*, will be allowed a step-up in basis on only half of the $900,000 gain; capital gains taxes will be owed on the balance. In this case, a $90,000 tax bill—20% of $450,000—comes due because of improper titling.

What if I held the same stock in my own name?

It would receive a 100% step-up in basis upon passing to your spouse, and could thus be sold, free of capital gains taxes. The same advantage would result if the stock was owned by your living trust.

I also avoid probate with a living trust, right?

Right. The expense, the delay, and the public disclosure of probate are eliminated.

How does titling affect the ability of creditors to attach assets in my estate, especially when they become the property of my heirs?

With regard to attachment of assets, you should consider not only creditors, but also the all-too-common consequences of divorce. Here are some guidelines as to the vulnerability of different types of assets:

Asset Vulnerability	
Ownership	**Attachability**
Individual ownership	Attachable
Joint property	Not attachable in some cases
Living trust	Attachable
Irrevocable trust	Not attachable
Family partnership	Only your interest is attachable

Are there any other plans I can make now regarding titling and estate tax planning?

Yes. Something I covered earlier bears repeating now from a different perspective. The 55% estate tax, which is the bedrock of our continuing discussion, is *not* an across-the-board rate. In fact, this "marginal rate" doesn't become effective until an estate is valued at $3 million or more.

Right. I remember.

I've also mentioned how, through the unlimited marital deduction, all solely owned assets may be bequeathed to your spouse estate tax-free.

I remember that, too.

Good. So, keeping both of these facts in mind, can you see how it might actually be a good thing to *pay estate taxes* when the first spouse dies?

No way!

Actually, yes! There's a lower marginal tax rate on assets under $3 million. In Chapter 12, we reviewed a detailed unified transfer tax schedule. Now let's look at a simplified version:

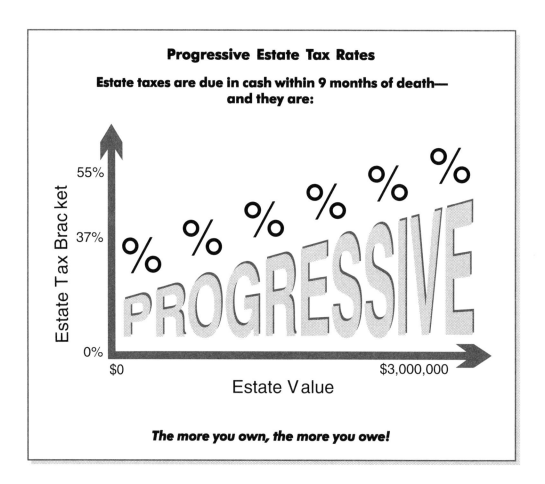

Progressive Estate Tax Rates

Estate taxes are due in cash within 9 months of death— and they are:

The more you own, the more you owe!

The point is that federal estate taxes are *progressive*: the higher the estate value, the higher the tax bracket, and, naturally, the higher the tax. Or as the chart so poetically puts it, "The more you own, the more you owe!"

Because of different rates for different size estates, it may not be to your best advantage to leave everything tax-free to your spouse. The two estates, now lumped together, may trigger a larger total tax bite for the next generation than separating the estates and paying estate taxes at the first spouse's death.

I think I see what you're saying, but let's do the math.

Good idea. Let's say you have an asset worth $3 million. If you leave it to your children at your death, they'll pay $1,079,500 in estate taxes after the 1999 exemption. If you leave it, along with the rest of your estate, to your spouse to pass on at his or her death, the $3 million would be taxed at 55%, resulting in estate taxes of $1,650,000. As you can see, the bracket shift avoids the additional $570,500 tax liability. In addition, the $3 million (or net $1.9 million) can grow free of estate taxes during your spouse's lifetime.

Therefore, you might want to consider holding just enough individually titled assets that *will* be subject to estate taxes at your death (because you leave them to someone other than your surviving spouse) to take advantage of lower tax rates on those assets. And don't forget that the same rule applies to your spouse. If your estate is substantial, you may likewise consider maintaining up to $3 million in his or her individual estate. If your spouse happens to die first, and those assets are left to the children, the taxes due would be calculated at a rate lower than the 55% maximum.

Chapter Summary

▪ Any asset—cash, land, stocks, etc.—must be *titled*: that is, it must have a legal owner (or owners). The owner can be a person or an entity, such as a trust. Careful consideration should be given to the type of ownership that will work best when an asset is passed to a new owner upon the death of the original owner.

▪ Three types of ownership, and the tax consequences of each, are:

• **Individual ownership** allows a step-up in basis, but may be subject to probate.

• **Joint ownership** allows step-up in basis for half of the property, and avoids probate.

• **Trust ownership** allows assets a step-up in basis and avoids probate *if* the trust is drafted properly and the asset is titled to the trust.

▪ Titling of assets may affect the ability of creditors to attach them:

• Individual ownership is attachable.

• Joint property is not attachable in some cases.

• Property held by a living trust is attachable.

• Assets held by an irrevocable trust are not attachable.

• If property is held by a family partnership, only *your* interest is attachable.

▪ In some cases, it may be advantageous to pay estate taxes at the death of the first spouse. Tax bracket shifting could result in tax savings. Careful examination of each spouse's individual estate is needed.

15

Gifting

"People's wealth and worth are very rarely related."

—Malcolm Forbes, 1919-90
American Publisher

In the preceding chapters, I introduced the benefits of gifting corporate assets to your successors, and presented methods for reducing the value of your estate without relinquishing control over the assets themselves.

Now I'm going to discuss the same principles relative to your personal estate. Personal estate planning requires the same amount of diligence as business succession planning, and offers equally important benefits. Many of the rules and strategies are, in fact, the same, but there are several additional techniques available only for personal interests.

How about a quick refresher course on the rules and strategies we discussed earlier?

Remember, first of all, that gifting an asset during your lifetime—rather than leaving it as a bequest—is far and away the wiser choice. Not only is the original asset out of the estate, but so is its appreciation. And although, percentagewise, the tax rates are the same, a gift tax paid today costs far less in the long run than an estate tax paid at death.

Next, let's quickly review the annual and lifetime gift allowances:

- the *annual gift tax exclusion* of $10,000 per person per year—to an unlimited number of recipients—which works on a "use it or lose it" basis;
- the *unified tax credit (lifetime exemption)*; and

- the *generation skipping transfer* (GST) *tax lifetime exemption* of $1 million per grandparent (which will be covered in this chapter).

Finally, a number of specialized techniques for shifting or reducing value were also covered previously. These techniques, as they apply to personal assets, will be reviewed in upcoming chapters. They include:

- *family limited partnerships*;
- *limited liability companies*; and
- *grantor-retained annuity trusts* (GRATs).

Gifting to charity and other strategies will be discussed as well.

Clear something up for me. I've heard that the lifetime exemption is for use after death only. Is this true?

Assuming that you don't need the assets during your lifetime, the answer is simply this: *it's not true.* If you give assets away during your lifetime, the tax you pay is *not* considered an additional taxable gift. Secondly, future appreciation occurs completely outside of your estate. For example, let's assume that you have an asset worth $1 million, which over the next several years grows to $2 million. If you leave the asset in your estate, the $1 million appreciation becomes part of your taxable estate. But if you gift the asset today, the appreciation occurs outside your estate, thus saving your heirs $550,000 in estate taxes.

Here's an even more dramatic example of how the creative use of gifting can benefit you and your heirs:

> *Granddaddy Mel will surely be remembered by future generations. With a net worth today of $15 million, the 80 year-old widower realizes that his daughter, grandchildren, and great-grandchildren might see very little of it if he doesn't plan properly. In fact, without proper planning, less than $3.7 million would be inherited by Mel's grandchildren after he and his daughter pass away.*
>
> *Mel's estate planning team proposes that he gift $5 million to his daughter now, paying the $2.5 million gift tax. This will, in effect, reduce the gift tax to 33%, because the gift tax itself is not considered*

taxable. The daughter, in turn, will gift $1 million of the original $5 million to an irrevocable life insurance trust for her children (Mel's grandchildren). The $1 million will be used to purchase a $7 million joint life second-to-die policy on Mel's daughter and her husband. Another $1 million will be placed in trust for her grandchildren (Mel's great-grandchildren), also funded with $7 million in second-to-die insurance. Both Mel's daughter and her husband will utilize their lifetime exemptions to minimize any gift tax on the $2 million gift.

By using his lifetime gift exemption, Mel is able to remove $7.5 million from his estate, save $2.5 million in estate taxes by making an early gift, and create $14 million of additional net assets. Over $17 million will survive Mel and his daughter, thus benefiting generations still unborn.

A reminder about life insurance is appropriate here. While it is true that proceeds to heirs are distributed free from *income taxes*, the death benefit itself, if left in the estate (that is, if it is owned by you personally at the time of your death), is subject to *estate taxes*. All of your planning, forethought, and good intentions will be carved up like the estate itself, if that one mistake is made.

Remember…

Your top priority is to put life insurance into a trust outside your estate!

Like Granddaddy Mel, I'd like my grandchildren to think fondly of me—and I'd prefer that they start now, not after I'm gone. But I'm confused by the regulations regarding gifts to grandchildren.

You have every right to be. Let's see if we can't clarify the issues a bit.

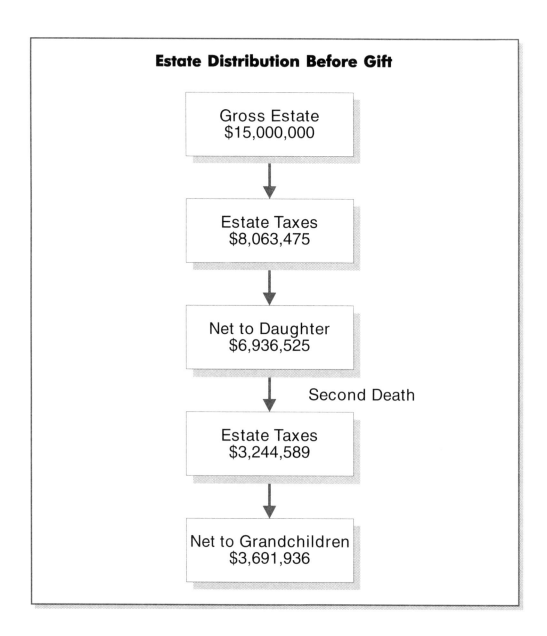

Estate Distribution Before Gift

Gross Estate
$15,000,000

Estate Taxes
$8,063,475

Net to Daughter
$6,936,525

Second Death

Estate Taxes
$3,244,589

Net to Grandchildren
$3,691,936

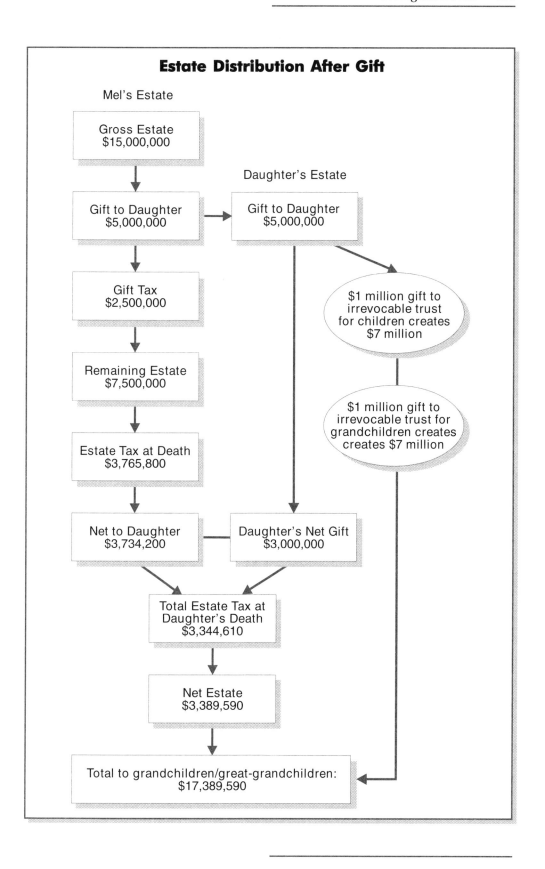

Estate Distribution After Gift

Mel's Estate

Gross Estate
$15,000,000

Daughter's Estate

Gift to Daughter
$5,000,000

Gift to Daughter
$5,000,000

Gift Tax
$2,500,000

$1 million gift to
irrevocable trust
for children creates
$7 million

Remaining Estate
$7,500,000

$1 million gift to
irrevocable trust for
grandchildren creates
creates $7 million

Estate Tax at Death
$3,765,800

Net to Daughter
$3,734,200

Daughter's Net Gift
$3,000,000

Total Estate Tax at
Daughter's Death
$3,344,610

Net Estate
$3,389,590

Total to grandchildren/great-grandchildren:
$17,389,590

The Generation Skipping Transfer (GST) Tax

This tax was instituted in 1976, retroactively repealed, then reinstated in 1986. Its intent, simply, was to counter the strategy of avoiding estate taxes imposed on bequests from one generation to the next by leaving large assets to grandchildren—a generation skipping transfer.

The GST tax is based on the value of property transferred to those persons two or more generations removed from the transferor, including grandchildren, great-grandchildren, grandnieces and grandnephews, and unrelated persons more than 37 years younger than the transferor. Such a recipient is called a "skip person."

The tax itself is a flat 55%, and it may be levied separately from any other applicable taxes on the same property that, as you'll see, can drastically dilute the asset.

Before we dilute, tell me about the GST tax exemption.

As a grandparent, you can gift up to $1 million without paying a GST tax. Like other exemptions, the amount doubles if you're married, allowing you and your spouse to shelter up to $2 million. This amount may be apportioned any way you choose—in a single lump sum or spread out over your lifetime—and any unused portion may be applied at your death.

However, gifted amounts *over* $1 million (in cash or valued assets such as stocks and real estate) are subject to normal estate taxes *and* the GST tax. But that's not all. The GST tax you pay is, itself, considered an additional gift, and as such is subject to the federal gift tax!

Sounds like a tax on a tax on a tax.

It is.

How can they do that?

They do it. And as a result, generation skipping transfers can carry an effective tax rate of up to approximately 80%.

What if I put the $1 million into a trust?

Many trusts are not exempt from the GST tax, and there are additional tax consequences that you and your advisors should consider carefully. But there is a powerful tax exempt trust, called a *dynasty trust*, that you can use to help shelter gifts to your grandchildren.

The dynasty trust has also been termed a "family bank," or even a "GST tax exempt trust." And like a bank account that's left to compound indefinitely, this irrevocable trust is designed to leverage its initial funding across multiple generations—*without taxation!* More than a source of capital appreciation, the funds can be used to enable many family necessities, from education to medical needs to building a home to building a business. All the good things your descendants may want to do can be made possible through the use of a dynasty trust. The money can even be used to help pay estate taxes if an estate support clause, which allows an exchange of assets in the estate, is included.

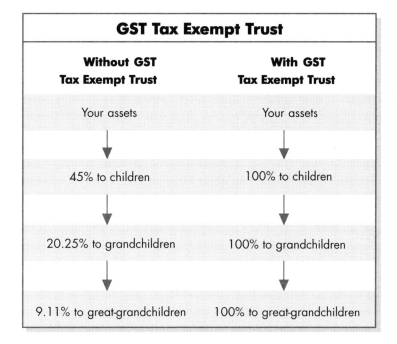

GST Tax Exempt Trust

Without GST Tax Exempt Trust	With GST Tax Exempt Trust
Your assets	Your assets
45% to children	100% to children
20.25% to grandchildren	100% to grandchildren
9.11% to great-grandchildren	100% to great-grandchildren

And the dynasty trust is exempt from the GST tax?

If it's established properly, yes. Contributions are protected, while appreciation grows free of GST taxes.

Speaking of protection, income from dynasty trust assets is also creditor- and divorce-proof.

One of the most popular kinds of dynasty trusts is also known as the *grandchildren's trust*. Here's an example:

Harry and Anne have five grandchildren. Since each grandparent is allowed to gift each grandchild $10,000 annually free from gift taxes, Harry and Anne together could gift $100,000 each year into a grandchildren's trust, which can be invested as the trustee sees fit.

But remember: there is a lifetime maximum of $1 million per person, GST tax-free, allowed as a trust contribution ($2 million for a married couple). Contributed assets over and above this amount are subject to double taxation: the dreaded GST tax.

Now let's take the same $100,000. If Harry and Anne are 65 years old, that contribution could fund second-to-die life insurance with a death benefit of perhaps $8 million—money that's not subject to GST taxes, not subject to estate taxes, not subject to income taxes, and not subject to capital gains taxes.

What if Harry and Anne have **ten** grandchildren?

Let's do the math. With our original family unit, the couple could gift $100,000 per year for 20 years—a total of $2 million in contributions. But if they have 10 grandchildren, Harry and Anne could, together, contribute up to $200,000 a year into the trust to reach the $2 million limit in 10 years. (By the way, the trust can also benefit *unborn* grandchildren and great-grandchildren, even though the number of living beneficiaries determines the annual gifting limit.)

Which situation allows the greater insurance benefit?

That depends on variables such as the age and health of the grandparents. The bottom line on a dynasty trust is that it's created to go on and on, building in value, preserving wealth, and avoiding taxes. Even though most states restrict the length of time that the trust may remain in existence (generally 80 to 110 years), your reputation as a patriarch would seem to be safe, indeed.

All this assumes that none of the principal is touched, and that insurance premiums are paid. What if the beneficiaries of the trust demand their share of the annual donation? Is this allowed?

Yes, under the unlikely name of *the Crummey power of withdrawal.*

But first, let's back up.

When you make a gift that's used to pay a premium on an insurance policy held in trust, you want the gift to be credited toward your *annual* $10,000 gift tax exclusion. However, only gifts of "present interest" qualify for the annual exclusion. In order for a gift of this sort to be valued as a gift of present interest, the beneficiaries must have the right to use it *now*—in the present. This is the "Crummey power," named after the family who in 1968 claimed that right in tax court...and won.

If a gift is *not* valued in this way, it's considered a gift of future interest, and as such, is deducted from your *lifetime* exemption. You're now a two-time loser: you've lost the annual exclusion (which cannot be carried over), and you've devalued your lifetime exemption.

To enable the Crummey power, trustees must send a letter to all beneficiaries whenever a deposit is made into the trust, which gives them a specified period of time to withdraw such funds. The beneficiaries, however, are not likely to exercise their power, as it would defeat the trustee's purpose in establishing the trust.

What if the letter isn't sent?

The contribution will either be subject to gift taxes, or be deemed a gift of future interest and deducted (as noted above) from your *lifetime* exemption rather than from your *annual* exclusion.

Chapter Summary

- Many of the same rules and strategies for gifting corporate assets apply to personal estate planning as well. These include:
  - *gifting* during your lifetime;
  - using your *annual gift tax exclusion*;
  - using your *unified credit (lifetime exemption)*; and
  - taking advantage of the *generation skipping transfer* (GST) *tax lifetime exemption.*

- While life insurance proceeds distributed to heirs are not subject to income taxes, the benefits *are* subject to estate taxes if the policy is left in the estate. Life insurance should be kept out of your estate by means of a trust.

- A *dynasty trust* can effectively shield its assets from taxation across multiple generations.

- Beneficiaries must be notified in writing of their right to take withdrawals from a trust. This right is known as the *Crummey power.*

16

Specialized Techniques

"Darwin didn't prove that survival is of the fittest. He really proved that survival is of the most **adaptable.***"*

—Jack Linkletter
American Entertainer

Many of the techniques used to effectively shelter gifts of business assets from taxes are equally as effective in the gifting of personal assets. But as I noted in the previous chapter, there are additional avenues open *only* to personal gifting. First, however, let's quickly review the basics of those techniques already covered.

Family Limited Partnership (FLP)

In an FLP, a grantor sets up the partnership and becomes its general (managing) partner, normally retaining 1% to 10% of the partnership interest. Limited (minority) partners receive their shares through gifts. A couple of notes: (1) the partnership may own all or a portion of a particular asset, and (2) the grantor may own the balance outside the partnership.

There may be gift taxes to pay on gifts to an FLP if the amounts are in excess of the applicable exemptions, but two significant discounts can be taken:

- a *lack of marketability discount*, because minority partners cannot easily sell their shares; and
- a *minority interest discount*, because these partners have few or no rights in determining the way the company is run.

These combined discounts can reduce the value of the asset by as much as 40%. The gifted assets are removed from the grantor's estate, while the grantor retains control.

Limited Liability Company (LLC)

An LLC offers the same benefits as an FLP, with the additional advantage of providing its members with protection from personal liability. Usually, there is one managing member (the parent) and a number of other members (the children).

Grantor-Retained Annuity Trust (GRAT)

In a GRAT, an income-producing asset is placed in trust, with the grantor receiving income in the form of annuity payments. At the end of the term, the beneficiaries assume ownership of the asset. The taxable gift amount is based on the remainder interest in the trust at the end of the trust period, which is a fraction of the actual current value.

If the GRAT is structured so that the total amount of the annuity payments over the term of the GRAT is high enough, the transfer is made with no gift tax consequences. This is referred to as a "zero-out GRAT."

But be sure to plan carefully: the asset will revert back to the estate if the grantor dies during the term of the trust. It wouldn't make sense to choose a 20-year term to zero-our your gift if your life expectancy is only 10 years, but life insurance can be used to hedge that bet.

In short, a GRAT gives you the opportunity to make a gift of business stock or real estate to your children with no estate taxes (assuming you live beyond the GRAT period) while continuing to receive an income from the asset.

Both the current gift and the annual payout will vary depending on your age, whether you've chosen a single life or joint life GRAT, and the valuation approach used. Different advisors take different approaches, so you'll definitely want to consult with yours before you set up a GRAT.

And now, let's talk about several additional specialized techniques for accomplishing the most tax-advantaged transfer of personal assets.

Qualified Personal Residence Trust (QPRT)

This specialized irrevocable trust holds a personal residence for a period of time, after which it's removed from the grantor's estate. The value of the asset is discounted in determining the value of the current gift.

The value of the property is divided into *present interest* (the right to live in the home for a fixed period) and *future interest* (commencing when the trust expires and its beneficiaries take possession). Government tables determine both values, and gift taxes are due only on the *remainder interest* at the time of gifting.

The following chart illustrates the taxable gift for a QPRT established at different age levels, and for different terms, for a $1 million home (which can be either a primary residence or a vacation home):

QPRT Trust				
	Taxable Gift*			
Term of Trust	**Age 50**	**Age 60**	**Age 70**	**Age 80**
10 years	$465,030	$414,370	$321,630	$166,630
15 years	305,350	245,880	148,490	42,330
20 years	182,690	133,270	53,590	6,880

*Assumes $1 million at 7% AFR (Applicable Federal Rate).

Let's say that you're now 60 years old. You've decided to give your $1 million home to your children, so you place the home in trust for 20 years. The value of the *gift* is only $133,270. In reality, however, the *home* will have appreciated to perhaps $3 million by the end of the trust period. So, because you moved the home out of your estate 20 years earlier, you may have saved your children $1,650,000 in estate taxes.

If you outlive the trust, you can continue to reside in the home by paying rent to your beneficiaries. This, too, may create a desirable situation, as you'll be transferring additional funds out of your estate in the form of rent payments, and at the same time continuing to enjoy the use of your property. Remember, though, that you won't be able to deduct your rent payments like you could mortgage payments. In addition, your beneficiaries will have to include the rent they receive from you as part of their taxable income.

If you die during the trust period, the value of the home at the time of your death reverts back into your estate. However, any exemption equivalent that was used to set up the trust is also restored to the estate, and becomes available to offset estate taxes. Pre-paid gift taxes are also credited against estate taxes.

In summary, if you survive the term of the QPRT, your mission is accomplished. If, on the other hand, you pass away while your home is in trust, your estate is no worse off than it would have been if a QPRT had never been established.

To further ensure that your estate will be protected from any potential tax burden, you can place a life insurance policy into a separate irrevocable life insurance trust for the period of the QPRT.

Is there a downside to using a QPRT?

Two cautions are warranted:

- You lose the stepped-up cost basis at death, which may result in higher capital gains taxes on the eventual sale of the home. However, it's better to pay a 20% capital gains tax than a 55% estate tax.

- You risk possible exposure to the GST tax if the trust's beneficiaries are skip persons (grandchildren, etc.) rather than children.

Sell Rapidly Appreciating Assets to Children

Up until now, the many strategies and techniques I've discussed for wealth preservation and appreciation all have one thing in common: they allow the patriarch/matriarch of the family to control the destiny of his/her money. Now, let's explore a transfer method that, in effect, surrenders the asset—and its control—completely.

But why would I even consider that?

Hold on…that's coming. Let's first meet Sally, who's done very well in real estate. Among her holdings is a parcel of land that she knows without a doubt will grow in value. She decides to sell the land to her son and daughter, paying the capital gains tax and removing the asset from her estate. She does so at a sale price lower than she might have received had she sold to an outside party, but not low enough to attract the attention of the IRS.

Why did Sally sell the land instead of gifting it? There may be several good reasons. Perhaps she has already used up her exemption, or maybe she wants this note receivable for her own security.

Let's say the land is worth $10 million, and it earns $1 million annually in leases. Had Sally simply bequeathed it to her children, they'd be hit with a $5.5 million bill in estate taxes. But by selling the property to the children for, say, $8 million at 6% interest, the kids pay $480,000 but take in $1 million each year.

Here are two other options:

Create New Business Entities

Be sure to think carefully about future investment opportunities. Instead of folding them into an existing entity—your current business or your personal estate—consider creating a new corporate entity outside your estate with your heirs as owners. If you design the new arrangement properly, you'll be able to pass along valuable assets without estate tax obligations. For example, if a new business opportunity were to arise, a mother could lend money to a new corporation owned by her children.

Lease Assets from Your Heirs

In a *passive family partnership* arrangement, the partnership owns an asset other than the family business itself, such as real estate. The partnership leases the asset to the business. One of the "partners" in this partnership, by the way, can be a trust set up for minor members of the family.

Proper design, as always, is critical. The arrangements of the lease—including term, payments, and ownership—must be carefully and properly defined to meet IRS guidelines for a fair and reasonable transaction.

We've oversimplified each technique in this chapter, of course. But the lesson here—and throughout the book—is not as simple as "give or sell everything before you die." It *is* as simple, however, as "get help and plan now." I can't emphasize enough the need for you and your advisors to study your estate and tax situations, consider all of the alternatives, and make sound, sensible, *proactive* decisions.

Chapter Summary

- Many techniques used to shelter gifts of *business* assets are also effective in gifting *personal* assets. Such techniques include:
  - family limited partnerships (FLP);
  - limited liability companies (LLC); and
  - grantor-retained annuity trusts (GRAT).
- Additional specialized techniques offering the most tax-advantaged transfer of personal assets include:
  - using a *qualified personal residence trust* (QPRT), which is effective for transferring property out of your estate and reducing gift and estate taxes;
  - *selling rapidly appreciating assets* to your children, which may result in a net profit after taxes;
  - creating new business entities; and
  - leasing assets from a passive family partnership.
- You and your advisors *must* study your estate and tax situations, and make sound, sensible, proactive decisions on the available alternatives.

17

Charitable Planning

"We make a living by what we get, we make a life by what we give."

—Sir Winston Churchill (1874-1965)

Another type of gifting involves gifts to charity. Whether intended to benefit public or private organizations, charitable gifts are 100% estate and gift tax-free. In addition, gifts made during your lifetime are income tax deductible up to allowable limits.

Charitable gifting, which provides personal and altruistic benefits, may take several forms:

- cash or appreciated property such as stocks or real estate;
- trusts, such as a *charitable remainder trust* (CRT); or
- foundations.

Cash Gifts

The easiest and most common form of gifting is a gift of cash or property, such as stock or real estate, to a public charity. Cash contributions are deductible up to 50% of adjusted gross income, and stock and real estate up to 30%. There are no complicated reporting procedures required with these types of contributions. The asset can be gifted outright to a specific organization, or to a philanthropic fund.

In addition to these types of outright bequests, there are instruments that offer advantages other than a current-year tax deduction.

Charitable Remainder Annuity Trust (CRAT) and Charitable Remainder Unitrust (CRUT)

Let's imagine the following desirable scenario. Some time ago, you purchased stock for $100,000 (your basis). It's now worth $1 million, but it pays no dividends. If you die with the stock still in your estate, it will be subject to taxation at 55%, for a whopping tax bill of $550,000. If you sell the stock during your lifetime, you'll qualify for a long-term capital gains tax rate of 20% on the $900,000 gain, resulting in a tax of only $180,000. But even if you were to sell the stock and pay the capital gains tax, the remaining $820,000 would still be subject to the 55% estate tax as it passes to your heirs. Either way, that's a lot of taxes.

But let's imagine instead that you've set up a *charitable remainder annuity trust* (or CRAT), and you donate the stock to it. The trust sells the stock for $1 million with *no capital gains tax*. It then invests the entire amount in income-producing assets. You take an annual payout of a fixed percentage of the gift. (This payout percentage will be determined by your age and prevailing IRS rates.) For example, with an 8% payout, the CRAT would pay you $80,000 a year for the rest of your life—and your spouse's life, if you set up the terms of the trust to provide for him or her in this manner. And at your (or your spouse's) death, the charity of your choice becomes the beneficiary of the assets. (Note that the Taxpayer Relief Act of 1997 mandates that the value of the remainder interest must be at least 10% of the fair market value of the original asset.)

In addition to avoiding the capital gains tax, you'll also realize some income tax savings on the $1 million donation (a deduction of approximately $170,000). And, there will be no estate taxes for your beneficiaries to pay at your death.

By donating your stock to a CRAT:

- a formerly non-income-producing asset provides you with a steady stream of income;
- the value of the asset has been removed from your estate; and
- your favorite charity benefits from your generosity.

A *charitable remainder unitrust* (or CRUT) works in a similar way, except that the method of investing and amount of payout to the donor is different.

In our previous scenario, the CRAT donor receives a fixed percentage of the *original* contribution—$80,000 a year based on an assumed 8% return on investment. The amount of the payout amount remains fixed regardless of the amount earned by the investment. A CRUT invests the same proceeds, but pays the donor a fixed percentage of the trust's *current* principal. As the interest compounds, the result is a continuously higher distribution—a sort of built-in cost-of-living increase. For example, if the payout was 8% a year but the trust earned 10%, the excess income can build up the principal to generate a higher income in the future. Take a look at this chart:

A Comparison of CRAT and CRUT Payouts		
	CRAT	**CRUT***
Year 1	$80,000	$80,000
Year 5	$80,000	$86,600
Year 10	$80,000	$99,600
Year 15	$80,000	$105,500
Year 20	$80,000	$116,500
Year 25	$80,000	$128,700
Year 30	$80,000	$142,000

*Assumes an earnings rate of 10% and a payout of 8%.

Is there a minimum or maximum amount on what is distributed back to the donor annually?

Yes. Each year, as a minimum, the trust must pay the donor the amount stipulated in the agreement. The 1997 Taxpayer Relief Act established a payout maximum of not more than either 50% of the initial fair market value of trust assets, or 50% of the annual value of trust assets, depending on the type of trust.

Also remember that these distributions to the "non-charitable beneficiary" (which is *you*) are subject to applicable income taxes.

Determining which type of trust will best suit your needs depends on a host of tax-related factors. Be sure to obtain the expert counsel of your advisors.

Who decides how and where the trust's assets will be invested?

The Board of Trustees of the charitable beneficiary can make the investments, but it is usually the donor who does so. When creating a private foundation, you and your spouse may elect to serve as its trustees, thus maintaining control over the investment of trust assets.

If you decide to serve as a trustee, however, be sure to keep in mind one vital aspect of how a trust works.

What's that?

The trust's assets should be *income-producing* assets. If not enough income is generated to meet the annual payout, you'll be forced to deplete the principal. This compromises the trust's ability to produce income in succeeding years, potentially leaving less remainder interest for the charity upon the trust's termination.

Do I have any other options?

Yes, and I'll describe one of them now.

Net Income with Make-Up CRUT (NIMCRUT)

Let's say you have assets you wish to contribute to a CRT. Although these assets are non-productive now, they have the potential to earn income in the future. A NIMCRUT distributes to you, the annuitant, the *lesser* of either the net income earned in a given year or a fixed percentage, within the limitations described above. A make-up account tracks the years when the fixed percentage has not been achieved. In the good years to come, these shortfalls are reimbursed. The result: trust corpus is preserved, and the annuitant receives the income when it's most needed.

Remember that with any CRT, assets within the trust will not pass to your beneficiaries, but you can more than compensate your family by establishing a *wealth replacement trust*.

Wealth Replacement Trust (WRT)

A WRT acts in concert with a charitable remainder trust, and functions as an irrevocable life insurance trust. By using funds produced by tax savings or from the annual income provided by the CRT, an individual or second-to-die life insurance policy may be taken out on you and/or your spouse. Proceeds distributed to the beneficiaries replace the original asset, free of estate, income, gift, and GST taxes.

To sum up, the charity of your choice gets the benefit of your donation, your children get the benefit of your forethought, and you and your spouse get income for life.

Charitable remainder trusts: they're a win-win-win situation.

What if we go even further—let's give the charity the income now, and save the remainder for my family at the back end of the trust.

What you've described is a *charitable lead trust* (CLT). Let's discuss the variations on that theme.

Charitable Lead Annuity Trust (CLAT) and Charitable Lead Unitrust (CLUT)

These trusts work, basically, the other way around: the *charity* gets the annual income produced during the term of the trust, with the remainder interest reverting back to the donor's *beneficiaries* at the end of that period. As the donor, you choose the trust's term—10 to 15 years, for example. Current income taxes are reduced, estate taxes are reduced or even eliminated, and your favorite charity or charities can put the money to work immediately.

Bear in mind, however, that there are potential gift, estate, and generation skipping transfer (GST) tax considerations about which you should consult your tax advisors.

Rather than designating a particular charity or charities, how can I contribute to—or even set up—a foundation?

In setting up a foundation, the first decision you'll need to make is which type you want: public or private.

Charitable Foundations: Public versus Private

A public foundation is community-based, and as such is out of an individual's total control. However, while the foundation controls the admin-

Private Foundations vs. Public Charities

	Private Foundation	Public Charity
Donor control	Donor is allowed complete control of organization.	Donor control is usually limited.
Public support	Generally, there is no public support.	Section 509(a)(2) and some Section 509(a)(1) organizations must meet public support requirements.
Investment income tax	1% or 2% tax is due on net investment income.	No tax is due on on investment income.
Deductibility of contributions	*Cash donations* are deductible up to 30% of donor's adjusted gross income (AGI).	*Cash donations* are deductible up to 50% of donor's AGI.
	Publicly traded stock is deductible at fair market value up to 20% of AGI.	*Publicly traded stock* is deductible at fair market value up to 30% of AGI. Donor may increase AGI limitation to 50% if he or she elects to deduct only cost or basis in the stock.
	Long-term capital gain property (closely held stock, real property, and similar capital assets) is deductible up to 20% of AGI (donor's cost or basis only).	*Long-term capital gain property* is deductible at fair market value up to 30% of AGI if it is related to the recipient's exempt function. The donor may increase AGI limitation to 50% if he or she elects to deduct cost or basis only. If tangible property is unrelated to the recipient's exempt function, only cost or basis is deductible, up to 50% of AGI.

istration of the gifts it receives, major donors can maintain a significant degree of interest by serving on the Board.

A private foundation is set up by an individual donor, or it can be created upon the donor's death. Often, the donor's children serve as trustees, and can conceivably draw salaries from and administer decisions for the foundation. Private foundations work well for people with large bequests.

Retirement accounts are excellent assets to bequest to either public or private foundations. A second-to-die life insurance policy held in an irrevocable life insurance trust can act as a WRT to offset net assets which would have been left to heirs if the charitable gift had not been made. A detailed comparison of private versus public charities is presented immediately preceding the Chapter Summary.

Private Foundations vs. Public Charities, Cont'd

	Private Foundation	Public Charity
Operating restrictions	Transactions are strictly regulated between private foundation and directors, officers, and substantial contributors.	Transactions between public charity and directors, officers, and substantial contributors is permissible if done "at arm's length."
	A minimum of 5% of net investment assets must be distributed annually for charitable purposes.	There is no minimum distribution requirement.
	Cannot own more than 20% of a single business, or hold investments that would jeopardize assets.	There is no limitation on control of a business or restriction on jeopardy investments, but state law fiduciary duties may apply.
	Additional recordkeeping and monitoring requirements are imposed when grants are made to individuals, taxable organizations, or other private foundations.	There are no corresponding restrictions, although Board is responsible for ensuring grants are used for exempt purposes.
	Violations of above-described operating restrictions are subject to excise taxes imposed on the foundation as well as the foundation managers.	No excise taxes apply except on political campaign expenditures.
Annual reporting	Form 990-PF requires detail on distributions, fees and salaries, investments, etc.	Form 990 requires less detail.

There are other alternatives, of course. Suffice it to say, it's all a matter of delving beneath the surface and studying your personal charitable goals and objectives.

Most important: the kinds of planning discussed in this book are *not* driven by your age, but rather by your net worth. More and more disposable wealth is being assumed by younger and younger people who see wills and trusts and insurance and charitable foundations as part of some far-in-the-future "to do" list.

The good news for younger people who have significant wealth is that funding future obligations *now* is relatively inexpensive. This is the time to put some of those plans into motion, instead of waiting until later when it costs more to do the same thing.

Your personal values can be perpetuated and your communities can be enhanced through the use of charitable bequests. We all want to make the world a better place because we've been in it. It's been said that it's not extinction man fears, but extinction with insignificance. When you establish a charitable trust, you have the satisfaction of knowing that you'll leave a significant legacy behind.

Chapter Summary

- Charitable gifts are 100% estate and gift tax-free. Gifts made during your lifetime are income tax deductible up to allowable limits.

- A *charitable remainder trust* (CRT) makes a charity the beneficiary of your donation upon your (or your surviving spouse's) death. The asset is removed from your estate, but you receive the income it produces throughout your lifetime. Versions of this trust differ in methods of investing and payout. They include:
  - the charitable remainder annuity trust (CRAT) ;
  - the charitable remainder unitrust (CRUT); and
  - the net income with make-up CRUT (NIMCRUT) .

- Assets within a CRT will not pass on to the donor's beneficiaries. A *wealth replacement trust* (WRT) functions as an irrevocable life insurance trust, using proceeds of an individual or joint life second-to-die insurance policy to replace the original asset, free of taxes.

- Income may be donated to charity during the donor's lifetime through a version of the *charitable lead annuity trust* (CLAT). With a CLAT, the charity receives annual income produced by the trust, with the remainder interest reverting back to the donor's beneficiaries at the end of a pre-determined term of years.

- There are a number of tax considerations to consider with regard to the many trust alternatives.

- Donating assets to private or public foundations is another way to make a worthy contribution with considerable benefits to the donor and his or her family. A retirement account can be an excellent funding vehicle.

- Personal values can be perpetuated and communities enhanced through the use of charitable bequests.

18

Qualified Plan Assets: The Double Tax Dilemma

"I'm proud to pay taxes in the United States. The only thing is, I could be just as proud for half the money."

—Arthur Godfrey, 1903-83
American Entertainer

Even the worst procrastinators—business owners or employees who have taken no steps to preserve a working lifetime of accumulated wealth—often sleep well at night, secure in the knowledge that their pension and retirement plans will provide not only for their old age, but also for their surviving spouses and heirs-in-waiting.

Sorry to ruin your sleep…but nothing could be further from the truth. As a matter of fact:

Retirement accounts are great to have during your lifetime, but they could possibly be the *worst* assets to leave behind.

I hate you.

Such is the messenger's lot. Nevertheless, let's talk about your pension and profit sharing plans. As you know, these accounts are funded with pre-tax dollars. It looks good going in, but when it comes out, it's time to pay the piper—or, more accurately, the IRS. If you die with the accounts still active, any funds left or passed to a non-spouse are subject to income *and* estate taxes.

The Impact of the Double Tax

Taxation on a qualified account:

Account balance		$3,500,000
Estate taxes	($1,925,000)	
Income taxes	(630,000)	
Total taxes		(2,555,000)
Net distribution		945,000
Net percentage		27%

Assumptions:
1. Estate tax equals account balance times estate tax rate (55%).
2. Income tax equals account balance minus estate tax, times income tax rate (40%).

Wow! All that work, all those savings, and my children will get only 27%?

Unless you plan otherwise.

What about my wife? Doesn't she get everything tax-free? If she uses all the money herself, why should we worry about double taxes?

These are good questions that, unfortunately, most people don't consider beforehand. Remember how we stipulated above that your pension and profit sharing plans were funded with *pre*-tax dollars? When withdrawals are made—whether by you, your spouse, or your great-grandchildren—income taxes come due. The only tax your spouse avoids is the estate tax.

Consider how such a situation might play out:

> *Upon John's death, his $1 million retirement fund passes to his wife Laura's estate. The account isn't subject to estate taxes until her death. Over the next ten years, Laura withdraws only the 10% annual interest/appreciation, paying income taxes on that amount. When Laura dies, she leaves the asset to Samantha, their only child.*
>
> *Samantha now owes the* double tax—*both estate and income taxes—on the $1 million account balance. Depending on her particular circumstances (the total size of the inherited estate and her individual tax bracket), the tax bite could very well leave*

*Samantha with as little as $270,000—a mere
27% of the original principal!*

Do both taxes have to be paid right away?

Under most circumstances, estate taxes are payable within nine months, and income taxes must be paid by April 15 of the year following the year in which the money is received. That's why I can't say enough about planning ahead—for yourself and for your heirs.

I believe you. So what other kinds of planning can I do?

You can set up a so-called *eternal IRA*, which is a multigenerational plan for spreading out distributions for as long as possible. Even though estate taxes are still payable at the time of your spouse's death, there are two key benefits to using an eternal IRA: (1) distribution of the plan balance—and the resulting income taxes—can be stretched out over the lives of your children, and (2) total distributions from the plan and the amount of plan assets preserved for future generations are greatly increased.

Sounds promising. Tell me what to do.

Here are the steps involved:

1. Name your spouse as the primary beneficiary of the IRA.
    *   Minimum distributions during both your lifetimes should be based on *joint* life expectancy. (Ideally, the owner's life expectancy should be recalculated each year.)
    *   The resulting minimum distribution may or may not be smaller than those based on your life alone. However, this is an important first step in preparing for the steps that follow.
2. At the owner's death, the surviving spouse rolls the IRA into a new account under the "spousal rollover" rules.
    *   No estate tax is triggered due to the unlimited marital deduction.
    *   The spouse can name the children as new beneficiaries of the plan balance. (A separate account should be set up for each child/beneficiary.)
    *   The spouse can elect a new method of calculating minimum distributions based on the joint life expectancy of the spouse

and child (maximum age difference is 10 years), again result-ing in lower minimum distributions.

3. At the spouse's death:

- Estate taxes are due on the plan balance.
- The minimum distribution is again recalculated, based on the child's life expectancy.

By using this strategy, plan distributions and the resulting income taxes are likely to be stretched out for 20 to 40 years beyond the original owner's life expectancy.

Wait a minute—where does the money come from to pay estate taxes when the spouse dies?

Money could be withdrawn from the account to pay the taxes. However, since the withdrawal itself would be subject to income taxes, this method is not usually recommended. Other estate assets can be used, but this may not be in the best interest of your heirs. I recommend joint life second-to-die life insurance as the most efficient funding alternative.

The chart on the next page illustrates how planning can turn your IRA into the instrument of security you intended it to be in the first place.

Also remember that, based on the amount and timing of your withdraw-als, you may be subject to additional penalties on your qualified assets.

If you withdraw too early...

Withdrawals of taxable qualified assets before age 59½ are subject to an additional 10% excise tax.

If you withdraw too little...

A 50% penalty is imposed for failure to withdraw a minimum amount of qualified assets each year beginning at age 70½.

How can I protect and preserve what's mine?

You don't want to pay the taxes? I don't blame you. How's this for a suggestion: get someone else to pay them—or replace them—for you.

Eternal IRA Example

Assumptions:

Current account balance	$2,000,000
Growth rate	8%
Minimum distribution start date	Age 70-1/2
Owner's current age	65
Owner's age at death	80
Spouse's current age	61
Spouse's age at death	84
Children's ages	
Child 1 (male)	36
Child 2 (male)	34
Child 3 (female)	32
IRA estate tax rate	55%
IRA income tax rate	40%

	Without Planning	With Eternal IRA
Current account balance	$2,000,000	$2,000,000
Owner's lifetime distributions (gross)	$2,059,715	$2,178,408
At owner's death:		
Account balance	$3,633,950	$3,513,869
Estate tax	—	—
Income tax	—	—
Spouse's lifetime distributions (gross)	$2,527,080	$2,001,710
At spouse's death:		
Account balance	$3,317,508	$4,099,966
Estate tax	$1,824,629	$2,254,981
Income tax	$597,151	— *
Net to children	$895,727 ***	$1,844,985 *
Each child's IRA beginning account balance	N/A	$1,366,655 **
Lifetime distributions (gross):		
Child 1	N/A	$2,523,341
Child 2	N/A	$2,829,861
Child 3	N/A	$3,169,552
Total	N/A	**$8,522,754**
Account balance at death:		
Child 1	N/A	$1,739,043
Child 2	N/A	$1,877,337
Child 3	N/A	$2,036,875 ***
Total	N/A	**$5,653,255**
Total gross distributions	**$4,586,795**	**$12,702,872**

   * Assumes funds needed to pay estate taxes come from estate assets other than IRA.
  ** Assumes spouse establishes separate IRAs for each child at owner's death.
*** Account balances subject to estate and income taxes as they pass to next generation.

How do I do that?

You can purchase insurance inside a wealth replacement trust. In our earlier example, John and Laura are over 59½, and they're able to begin withdrawing retirement funds with no penalties. By taking withdrawals, paying the income tax, and putting the net income into an irrevocable trust to purchase second-to-die life insurance, money is quite literally *created* to cover whatever costs the couple specifies. It's that easy.

Insurance can accomplish the exact goals you've just specified: *protecting and preserving what's yours.* Note, too, that a second-to-die policy, because it covers two lives, offers rates that are substantially lower than a standard policy on one life.

Upon the death of the second person covered, the death benefit would ideally be used to pay all estate taxes—and be exempt from both income and estate taxes itself. The bottom line: insurance premiums paid from a trust *outside* your estate pay the taxes *on* your estate.

Let's see what it takes to provide $1 million utilizing a joint life second-to-die policy. Here's how it works when John and Laura are each 60 years old, and then when they're 70 years old.

Joint Life Second-to-Die Insurance				
Sample Costs for $1,000,000*, Male and Female age 60				
	Annual Premium	**Years Payable**	**Total Outlay**	**Net Present Value of Total Outlay at 7%**	**Internal Rate of Return at Life Expectancy (25 Years)**
Traditional whole life**	22,905	10	229,050	172,136	7.88%
Whole life with 25% term	19,710	9	177,390	137,404	8.47%
Whole life with 50% term	16,515	11	181,665	132,509	8.71%
Universal life:					
10 pay	19,988	10	199,880	150,214	8.04%
15 pay	14,655	15	219,825	142,820	8.42%
20 pay	13,268	20	265,360	140,199	8.64%

*All costs and values shown are for illustrative purposes only. Actual costs and values will vary depending on multiple factors, including age, health, product chosen, and prevailing rates.
**At life expectancy, total death benefit is $1,111,141.

To translate: the 60-year-olds can transfer approximately $200,000 (or approximately $20,000 a year for 10 years) to deliver $1 million of assets totally tax-free into an irrevocable trust that provides a guaranteed amount to their heirs for paying estate taxes. The internal rate of return works out to be approximately 8% after taxes, which currently is better than cash or bonds. It may not yield as high a return as the stock market or real estate over the long term, but it is *certain* and *guaranteed* to be paid when death occurs (the time that the taxes are triggered).

Two 70-year-olds would be required to transfer approximately $350,000 to provide that same $1 million. Obviously, the earlier the insurance is purchased, the less costly it is. Also, health is generally better at a younger age, which will keep the cost of the policy down.

As you can see, you've got some important decisions to make about your retirement assets. Think about these questions before you finalize your plans:

- What do I want to happen to my retirement accounts when I die?
- Do I want my children to be liable for huge taxes, which will be due at once?
- Can I stretch my income out over a period of time?

Joint Life Second-to-Die Insurance Sample Costs for $1,000,000*, Male and Female age 70				
	Annual Premium	Years Payable	Total Outlay	Net Present Value of Total Outlay at 7%	Internal Rate of Return at Life Expectancy (17 Years)
Traditional whole life**	40,435	9	363,915	281,884	8.55%
Whole life with 25% term	34,785	10	347,850	261,417	8.57%
Whole life with 50% term	29,135	11	320,485	233,767	9.57%
Universal life:					
10 pay	36,703	10	367,030	275,832	8.13%
15 pay	27,130	15	406,950	264,395	8.71%
20 pay	23,338	20	466,760	243,804	9.61%

*All costs and values shown are for illustrative purposes only. Actual costs and values will vary depending on multiple factors, including age, health, product chosen, and prevailing rates.
**At life expectancy, total death benefit is $1,080,520.

▪ If I have enough retirement assets, could I gift something to a charity or foundation?

We finish this chapter, then, the way it began, with one addition:

Retirement accounts are great to have during your lifetime,

but could possibly be the worst assets to leave

behind...*without proper tax planning*.

Chapter Summary

▪ Because retirement accounts are funded with pre-tax dollars, they will be subject to payment of both income and estate taxes at your death, resulting in a loss of as much as 73% of the account's balance. If your spouse inherits the account, he or she will not be responsible for the estate taxes, but at his or her death, your children will owe both income and estate taxes on the balance.

▪ An *eternal IRA* is a multigenerational plan for spreading out distributions—and the resulting taxes—for as long as possible, thus maximizing the value of the account.

▪ Based on the amount and timing of withdrawals, additional penalties on qualified plan assets may be due.

▪ A second-to-die life insurance policy can be an efficient vehicle for paying taxes on retirement accounts.

19

Funding Taxes

"Government today sits as an invisible partner
of every company, every family, and every
individual in the country."

—William L. Wearly
CEO, Ingersoll-Rand Corporation
International Division

The dreaded estate tax bill has come. Now what? If measures have not been taken to eliminate, delay, or reduce them, these taxes may destroy an existing or emerging family legacy. You've got the ball and the clock's ticking: it's time to call the play.

The good news is, there are a number of options available. The bad news is, the wrong choices may put your heirs in disadvantageous positions for many years to come.

The illustration on the following page displays the various options for funding estate taxes.

Cash/Liquid Assets

If your heirs can raise enough cash without imperiling the estate or their own financial stability, they can simply pay the tax bill and move on.

But this is easier said than done. The biggest problem is that most people don't have enough cash lying around to pay the taxes—they can find better things to use it for, and they do. Another problem is that any cash earmarked for taxes would be included in the estate, and accordingly, subject to estate taxes itself.

How Families Pay Estate Taxes

Cash on Hand

Liquidating Assets

Planned Savings

Borrowing

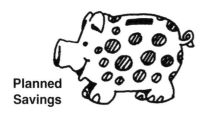

Section 303 Stock Redemption

Section 6166 Government Loan

Life Insurance

Also, consideration must be given to whether using liquid assets to pay taxes might cause a financial hardship for your heirs.

Planned Savings

Theoretically, it's possible to set up a sinking fund to pay estate taxes, but there are problems involved with such a plan. One is that an unexpected early death could cut short the time needed to build up enough money. Also, even if you have the foresight and gifting ability to set up the fund outside your estate in order to avoid estate taxes on the fund itself, there will be income taxes to pay on fund income, so the amount you need to set aside is greater.

Perhaps the biggest problem with planned savings, however, is maintaining the discipline necessary to set the money aside, and to leave it alone.

Liquidating Assets

Selling their inheritance should *not* be your family's first option. When your heirs are forced to liquidate assets to pay estate taxes, they face the emotional trauma of selling off what took you—their parent—a lifetime to accumulate. Also, there may be shock and resentment when they realize they'll be receiving only 50, 40, or even 30 cents on the dollar from a forced sale.

Although the tax bill will probably be lower after some of the assets are sold and the estate's ultimate value is reduced accordingly, this option should nevertheless remain a last resort.

Bank Loans

Borrowing money to pay transfer taxes is a better solution, but not by much.

To begin with, lending institutions may not recognize the stability of the next generation, so they may not approve a loan. And even if a loan is granted, the collateral required may be part—or all—of the family business itself.

Second, a loan merely substitutes one creditor for another—a bank for the government.

And finally, at what cost is the substitution being made? Principal plus interest compounded over a number of years can be very expensive. Let's do the math:

Bank Loan		
Term of Loan	$1 Million at 8%*	$1 Million at 10%*
5 years	$1,216,583	$1,274,822
10 years	$1,455,931	$1,585,800
15 years	$1,720,174	$1,934,289
20 years	$2,007,456	$2,316,000
25 years	$2,315,448	$2,726,100
30 years	$2,641,554	$3,159,259

*Payments made monthly

At 8% over 30 years, your heirs would have to earn $2.6 million *after income taxes* to pay off a $1 million loan!

IRS Section 303: Stock Redemption

Section 303 is a provision of the Internal Revenue Code that permits a corporation to redeem stock from an estate to pay estate taxes. There are some qualifications:

1. The stock being redeemed must be part of the gross estate, and must comprise more than 35% of the estate's adjusted gross value.

2. Proceeds from the redemption must not exceed the total of estate and inheritance taxes, plus funeral and administrative expenses.

If these qualifications are met, Section 303 may be elected to raise needed cash, free from capital gains taxes. How? The seller receives a step-up in basis for the stock equal to the sales price. As such, there is no gain for tax reporting purposes: it's an even trade. As for the corporation, the value of the stock being redeemed is fully discounted as well, with no income taxes due.

Section 303 sounds like a very viable way to solve the cash flow problem with no downside—or is there one?

Consider the case of Elaine.

> *Both Elaine and her partner have children who work in the business. When Elaine dies, her children find they must elect Section 303, redeeming part of their mother's stock to pay estate taxes. As a result, Elaine's children no longer own 50% of the company; instead, they're now minority stockholders. The balance of power has changed because Elaine's family didn't have an adequate plan.*
>
> *If the company is undervalued at the time of Elaine's death, her children would have to sell off even more stock than they anticipated to meet expenses, decreasing their ownership position even further.*
>
> *Or, if Elaine happens to die during a particularly bad business year, the company might not even have the cash available to carry out the transaction.*

Hmmm…Section 303 may not be the best bet after all. But I've heard there's a way to actually get credit extended to the estate by the government.

In a manner of speaking, that's true. You're referring to Section 6166.

IRS Section 6166: Installment Payments

Section 6166 of the Internal Revenue Code provides for a quasi-variable-rate installment loan. While there are some similarities to Section 303, there are also some significant and consequential differences.

Let's talk first about how your family might qualify. As with Section 303, the business interest must represent at least 35% of the adjusted gross estate value. There are some additional provisions, however. Multiple businesses may be included, provided that 20% or more of each business' value is contained in the estate, and that the combined interests total 35% or more of the entire adjusted gross estate. In addition, family members may combine their individual portions of ownership to satisfy the 35% minimum.

If these and certain other qualifications are met, a deferral of estate taxes may be arranged—but not for *all* of the estate taxes. The program is limited to those taxes owed on the *business* portion of the estate. So if business interests total 40% of your estate, you may defer only 40% of the taxes.

If we meet all of these qualifications, what are the terms of the loan?

The executor of your estate may defer payment of the tax for five years, paying only the interest during this period. Thereafter, the tax is paid in equal installments over the next ten years. The loan rate is 2% on the first $1 million of the value of the business in excess of the exemption equivalent. (The $1 million figure will be adjusted for inflation starting in 1999). Interest on the balance is payable at a special Section 6166 rate: 45% of the rate applied to tax underpayments. For example, 45% of a 9% underpayment rate is 4%. Both rates are calculated on a daily compounded basis, and interest payments are not deductible.

You must also confirm that your state's probate court will allow such a deferral in the first place. And note, too, that the executor assumes *personal* liability for all payments—principal and interest.

Section 6166 can provide needed relief for a family facing a large tax bill without the liquid assets to pay it. Consult your tax advisor about the applicability of Section 6166.

Is there anything else I should consider?

Bear in mind that all of the alternatives discussed here refer only to taxes due on that portion of the estate that isn't going directly to the surviving spouse. As I've mentioned, under the unlimited marital deduction, your estate would pass tax-free to your spouse, deferring taxes until his or her death.

So what is the **best** way to pay estate taxes?

The best method for paying estate taxes is usually life insurance, if it's available at a reasonable cost. Some of the advantages are:

- It's an asset that generally pays out more than you put in—often many times more.

- It's there, in full and immediately, when you need it.

- It can be clearly and legally kept out of your estate in a variety of ways customized to meet your family's specific needs.

- It's a form of forced savings, and as such, is an orderly and systematic vehicle with which to meet your needs and goals.

- It creates wealth where there isn't wealth, and liquidity where there isn't liquidity.

The chart on the next page summarizes the costs per dollar of the various funding options.

Listed below are the advantages and concerns associated with each method.

- Cash on hand
  - Advantages include: it's easy to use; it's always available; and there is no interest to pay.
  - Concerns are: there may not be enough cash; it's subject to estate taxes; there may be better uses for it; and creditors may want it.

- Planned savings
  - Advantages include: it's easy to use; it's always available; and there's no interest to pay.
  - Concerns are: there may not be enough time to save; income taxes may impede growth; it's subject to estate taxes; there may be better uses for the money; and creditors may want it.

- Liquidating assets
  - Advantages include: there is no need to save during life; and there is no interest to pay.
  - Concerns are: your heirs may not be able to find buyers; they may not be able to get full value; the buyer may not have all of the money; the sale may take too long; assets may be subject to estate taxes; the family may want to keep the asset; and there is a cost involved in selling assets.

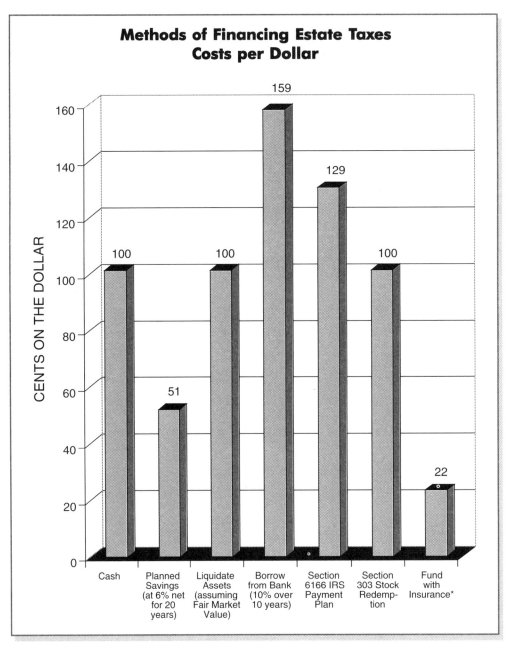

Methods of Financing Estate Taxes
Costs per Dollar

*At age 60. All costs and values shown are for illustrative purposes only. Actual costs and values will vary depending on multiple factors, including age, health, product chosen, and prevailing rates.

- Bank loans

  - Advantages include: there is no immediate outlay; it uses other people's money; and there is a single sum transfer.

  - Concerns are: your heirs may not be able to find a lender; interest charges can be high; it may be difficult to pay back the principal; loan payments may impede lifestyle; and there may be a lien on assets.

- IRS Section 303: stock redemption

  - Advantages include: it uses corporate assets; there are no capital gains on the stock sale; and there is no interest to pay.

  - Concerns are: your estate may not meet the requirements; it's not available for non-business assets; and your family's ownership in the business may be altered in ways you never intended.

- IRS Section 6166: installment payments

  - Advantages include: there is no immediate outlay; it uses the government's money; interest only is payable for four years; and principal and interest is payable for 10 years.

  - Concerns are: your estate may not meet the requirements; it's not available for non-business assets; if a payment is missed, the entire balance becomes due; the IRS puts a lien on the business; it may be difficult to pay back the principal; and installment payments can outlast the business.

- Life insurance

  - Advantages include: funding is guaranteed; benefits are paid income tax-free; cash accumulations are tax deferred; and there are flexible outlay options.

  - Concerns are: it requires annual premiums; a medical exam is required for qualification; and if you wish benefits to be paid estate tax-free, you can't own the insurance.

Chapter Summary

- There are a variety of options available to fund your estate tax bill. The choice must be made with utmost care and forethought. The available options include:
  - cash on hand;
  - planned savings;
  - liquidating assets;
  - bank loans;
  - IRS Section 303: stock redemption;
  - IRS Section 6166: installment payments; and
  - life insurance.
- Life insurance is the best way to pay estate taxes if the cost is reasonable.

20

What to Expect from Your Advisors

"Intelligence is knowing what you don't know.
Wisdom is knowing who to ask. Success is the
courage to do so."

—Anonymous

So…do business succession and personal estate planning now seem a bit less intimidating?

Well, let's just say I'm not as out of breath hearing about it as I was earlier.

Good. You've come to realize that there are many problems that come with the territory, but you now also know that there are just as many techniques to solve them. But how do you go about identifying your own issues and implementing solid solutions?

*I think it's more a matter of how **we** go about it—meaning me and my team of advisors, as you've suggested.*

That's very true. The success and survival of your family business may quite literally depend on the professionals you choose, but selecting your advisors can often be daunting. Who do you call in addition to those already on your team? How do you choose the right people, and what should you expect from them?

Every business owner needs help solving problems that are obvious and ongoing. But what about problems you may not even know you have? You may have outgrown your existing advisors, for instance, without realizing it.

Or even more likely, you may not know any professionals who specialize in the areas of business and wealth transfer planning.

There are perhaps a dozen different types of advisors a family business owner can hire. The first one that generally comes to mind is the *attorney*. An attorney can set up a corporation; draft documents such as buy/sell agreements, wills, and trusts; and can provide general tax and estate planning advice.

The second most common advisor is the *accountant*, who is responsible for preparing tax returns and financial statements, and for providing general business advice.

The *insurance professional* helps determine the need for insurance. He or she selects the right companies and products to guarantee income to the family, pay estate taxes, fund buy/sell agreements, and purchase products such as keyperson insurance, disability, long-term care, hospitalization, dental coverage, etc. The insurance professional can act as a catalyst for succession planning, estate planning, retirement planning, and employee benefits planning.

The *banker* generally makes loans, sets up lines of credit, and provides information on financial instruments (CDs, tax-free money market accounts, etc.).

The *trust officer* generally manages trust assets, and can help set up trust accounts during the donor's lifetime, as well.

Financial planners can help establish investment programs. Financial planners often sell products such as mutual funds or insurance. They may be stockbrokers, insurance professionals, bankers, or accountants, all of whom can sell financial products.

The *stockbroker* generally buys and sells stocks and can select money managers.

The *investment banker* can help sell a business or buy a new business. They can also raise venture capital through public or private placement of stock or debt, and are experienced in valuing businesses.

The *appraiser* can value a business for gift purposes, divorces, ESOPs, or potential sale. There are stand-alone appraisers, but banks and accounting firms can also perform this function.

The *family business consultant* can address family business concerns, such as designing compensation packages, developing successors, drafting transition plans, setting up outside boards, setting up governance programs, and facilitating general strategic planning. Again, these planning areas cross many disciplines and can involve many different kinds of advisors.

The *psychologist* can help solve relationship problems or conflicts in a business.

Finally, the *executive search specialist* assists in recruiting the proper candidates for key positions.

As you can see, there are very specific responsibilities with which each type of advisor is charged.

But how do I know that my team members are more than just experts in their field—that they're really helping me plan for my family's well-being after I'm gone?

You're right. There's too much at stake to depend on credentials alone. Advisors need to be perpetual students, learning and practicing the latest regulations and techniques. They need to be resourceful on their clients' behalf. And they need to be able to communicate well, not only with their clients, but also with other members of the advisor team in a collaborative way.

What kinds of things should I look for when interviewing potential team members?

There are a number of important considerations that should influence your decision.

- ☑ Is there positive chemistry between you and the prospective advisor? Do you trust—and have confidence in—him or her?
- ☑ Does the advisor have experience working with businesses like yours?
- ☑ Is the advisor highly successful in his or her field?
- ☑ Does he or she stay current on changing regulations and techniques?
- ☑ Is the person suited for the role you need filled?
- ☑ Is the advisor responsive to your calls and accessible when needed?

If your advisors are well chosen, they can be of inestimable service in:

- capitalizing on opportunities;
- anticipating and solving problems;
- resolving conflicts;
- providing practical solutions; and
- helping to implement action plans.

Chapter Summary

- There are at least 12 different types of advisors with whom you can work: attorney, accountant, insurance professional, banker, trust officer, financial planner, stockbroker, investment banker, appraiser, family business consultant, psychologist, and executive search specialist.

- Consideration must be given to more than just an advisor's credentials. They should be:
  - perpetual students, staying current on the latest regulations and techniques;
  - resourceful on their clients' behalf;
  - able to communicate well; and
  - able to collaborate well with other advisors.

- Considerations in selecting advisors include:
  - chemistry between you and the prospective advisor;
  - experience with businesses like yours;
  - success in his or her field;
  - suitability for the role; and
  - responsiveness and accessibility.

- A well-chosen advisor can help you to:
  - capitalize on new opportunities;
  - anticipate and solve problems;
  - resolve conflicts;
  - provide practical solutions; and
  - implement action plans.

Conclusion

"Don't try to die rich, but live rich."

—Thomas Bird Mosher, 1852-1923
American Publisher

You've spent a lifetime building your business and accumulating assets while raising your family. Things have happened so fast (so it seems) while you've been busy putting out the "brush fires" of business problems and daily living.

Now, just when you're looking to ease up a little bit, I've presented you with a "forest fire" that needs to be brought under control. But like all of the other problems you've faced, these business succession and estate planning "fires" *can* be controlled by using strategies and tools made possible by the same government that will be seeking to collect its share of your assets in the form of taxes.

Business succession planning requires considerable effort on your part—in the form of leadership, participation, and cooperation. But if it's done properly, it can be a real exclamation point of achievement to mark the end of your career.

Likewise, wealth transfer planning can provide you with great satisfaction. Making strategic decisions about *who* gets *what*, and *when* they get it, helps to ensure that your children, grandchildren, and great-grandchildren achieve and maintain financial security. Additionally, your favorite charities and other altruistic causes can be perpetuated long after you're gone.

I hope this book has provided you with the necessary insight, practical tools, and motivation to get started on putting your affairs in order and making the best possible provisions for those you care about: your family, employees, and charities. In this sense, *Passing the Bucks* means more than just distributing assets. If you plan carefully, the fruits of your life's work can make a positive, significant, and meaningful difference for generations to come.

Appendix One:

"TEN COMMANDMENTS" FOR WEALTH PRESERVATION

"Ten Commandments" for Wealth Preservation

Few are the successful businesspersons who do not set, maintain, and revise goals. But your efforts can't stop there…or your estate might end there.

True lasting financial success consists of three elements: accumulation, preservation, and distribution of wealth. If we think of the *accumulation* and eventual *distribution* as firmly-rooted trees, we can envision *preservation* as the hammock that connects them. Only when all three elements exist can we relax.

The following "ten commandments" are goals for keeping as much of your hard-earned wealth as possible. Each is do-able, and each has a vital place in your ultimate long-term plan: to provide for your family and business for generations to come.

1. Create and maintain proper will and trust documents.
2. Properly title assets to fully utilize estate tax credits.
3. Provide security for your family in the event of your retirement, disability, or death.
4. Make use of charitable gifting and annual and lifetime gifting exemptions.
5. Reduce your estate taxes to the minimum allowed by law.
6. Create a way to pay your estate taxes with pennies on the dollar.
7. Review the amount, type, and structure of your insurance portfolio.
8. Make certain your investment portfolio is properly diversified.
9. Prepare a succession plan for your business.
10. Create a cost-effective executive benefit plan to reward and retain key employees.

Appendix Two:

SAMPLE BUSINESS SUCCESSION AND ESTATE PLANNING SITUATIONS

Example 1:
Business Succession Planning

The situation:

- Steve, age 65, owns a business worth $3,000,000.

- He has two sons who work in the business.

- Steve owns his business' building. Rental income, plus his business assets, are sufficient to take care of Steve and his wife.

The issues:

- How to pass the business to the sons tax-free.

- How to retain a controlling interest in the business for at least ten years.

The solution:

- Create a family partnership, giving away $2 million in business interest to the sons.
  - The $2 million in equity can receive a minority discount of between 20 and 40%, reducing it to $1.2 to $1.6 million.
  - The $1.2 million is within the unified limit for lifetime gifts, so no gift tax would be due.

- Create a grantor-retained annuity trust (GRAT) for the remaining $1 million in equity.
  - Calculate the annuity payments to Steve so as to leave $0 equity in the GRAT after 10 years.
  - Because the remainder interest in the trust is $0, there is no gift tax due on the transfer.
  - Steve's income from the GRAT can be used to maintain his lifestyle or to fund any remaining estate tax liability.

- If Steve dies before the final payment is made, the assets are brought back into his estate as if the GRAT had never existed.

The result:

- If Steve survives the term of the GRAT, the entire $3 million is transferred to the next generation tax-free.
- Even if Steve dies before the end of the term:
    - $2 million in assets has still been transferred tax-free due to gift tax exemptions and discounts.
    - Life insurance could be used to fund the potential estate tax liability.

Example 2: Business Succession Planning

The situation:

- Ned owns a car dealership with a book value of $2 million and a fair market value of $8 million. He has $2 million in other assets.

- His two children work in the business and he plans to have them operate the business after his death.

- At death, Ned plans to leave the business to a revocable trust controlled by Corinne, his wife. The children would then inherit the business from Corinne at her subsequent death.

The issues:

- Leaving the business to Corinne postpones the estate tax until her death. At that time, the IRS would most likely use the fair market value of $8 million to calculate estate taxes on the business, so an estate tax of $4.6 million (based on the $10 million total estate), plus 55% on any future appreciation, could be due.

- The children will work for Corinne during her lifetime.

- Corinne's income will be dependent on her children's success in running the business.

- There may not be sufficient liquidity to pay the estate taxes.

The solution:

- Ned enters into a buy/sell agreement with his children to sell the business to them at his death.

- The agreement specifies a price (by formula) which is close to book value.

- The agreement is funded through a split-dollar life insurance policy for $3 million.

- The insurance proceeds pass to the children, income and estate tax-free.
- Corinne sells the business to the children, capital gains and estate tax-free.
- Second-to-die coverage can be obtained to fund the estate taxes (approximately $2 million) at Corinne's death.

The result:

- Valuation problems with the IRS are minimized because the buy/sell agreement pegs a value for the business at Ned's death, rather than many years later at Corinne's death.
- The children own the business at Ned's death.
- The estate tax drops from $4.6 million (on Ned's entire estate, due at Corinne's death) to approximately $2 million (on the assets remaining to Corinne—$3 million from the buy/sell agreement and $2 million from Ned's other assets).
- Corinne has an independent source of income and is not dependent on her children's success in running the business.
- All future appreciation of the business is removed from Corinne's estate.

Example 3:
Retirement Income

The situation:

- Greg, a 53-year old businessman, recently purchased a controlling interest (70%) in a manufacturing company with approximately 50 employees. There are two minority shareholders, ages 31 and 35.

- Greg had worked for large manufacturing companies for 25 years, but had accumulated virtually no retirement assets due to reorganizations, bankruptcies, and other events. He is very concerned about his own retirement and the security of the two minority shareholders.

The issues:

- Use of a qualified plan would be costly, as it would require coverage of all employees.

- Greg's age requires a vehicle that will provide rapid cash buildup.

The solution:

- Draft a non-qualified deferred compensation plan for the three shareholders.

- Fund the plan with a specially designed insurance contract to achieve tax-free cash buildup with minimal insurance protection.

- The plan can be funded through the corporation.
  - The cash value is a corporate asset and is accumulated on the balance sheet tax-free.
  - The corporation receives a tax deduction as the benefits are paid.
  - The corporation recovers the cost at the employees' deaths via the insurance proceeds.

The result:

- For Greg, $38,000 a year is contributed for 13 years.

  - The plan provides Greg with a $100,000 annual retirement benefit for 15 years, based on current interest rates.

  - The death benefit on his plan is $1,200,000, which can fund a death buyout and reimburse corporate costs for the retirement plan.

- For each of the minority stockholders, $5,000 a year is contributed until they reach age 65.

  - This provides an annual retirement benefit of $91,000 for 15 years to each shareholder (at current interest rates).

  - The death benefits can, again, fund a death buyout and/or reimburse corporate costs.

Example 4: Estate Planning and the Second Marriage

The situation:

- Fifty-five year old Ken and Susan, his second wife, have an estate totaling $5 million.
    - $2 million of the assets are owned by Ken personally.
    - $1.6 million are owned jointly by Ken and Susan.
    - $1.4 million is in the form of life insurance on Ken's life, payable to Susan at his death.
- Ken has two children from his first marriage, and Susan has a son from a previous marriage.
- Ken would like his children to get $2 million each, and Susan's son to get $1 million, after he and Susan are both gone.
- At Susan's death, she plans to leave all of her assets to a trust for her son.

The issues:

- If Ken dies before Susan, she can leave both her own assets, the life insurance, and the jointly owned assets to her own son.
    - Her son could receive approximately $3 million of the $5 million total.
- Ken's own children may receive only a small portion of his estate, with the majority going to Susan's son.
    - Ken's children could receive as little as $1 million each.
- If Ken leaves fewer assets to Susan, she may not have sufficient income to maintain her standard of living.
- There is no funding to pay the estate taxes.

The solution:

- Make Ken's children the beneficiaries of his life insurance policies and transfer the policies to an irrevocable life insurance trust.
  - The trust can also purchase a joint life second-to-die policy to fund the estate taxes.
- Leave the exemption amount ($650,000 in 1999, increasing to $1 million in 2006) to the trust for Ken's children.
  - This will allow Ken to take advantage of the lifetime exemption.
- Retitle $600,000 of jointly owned assets to be owned by Ken's trust, leaving $1 million to be jointly owned.
- Leave the remainder of Ken's assets to a qualified terminable interest property (QTIP) trust for Susan.
  - Susan is entitled to the income from the trust during her lifetime.
  - She may access the principal in the trust under specified circumstances.
  - The trust assets pass to Ken's children at her death.
- Susan's assets can still pass to her son at her death.

The result:

- If Ken dies first, estate taxes will be deferred until Susan's death, and funded by a joint life second-to-die policy.
- Susan will have adequate income throughout her lifetime from the trusts Ken set up.
- Ken's children will receive the majority of his assets.
  - Approximately $4 million will pass to his children.
  - Susan's son will still receive the $1 million inheritance from her assets.

Example 5:
Survivor Income Needs

The situation:

- Paul, a business owner, has an estate worth $5 million, including business assets worth approximately $2 million.

- Paul is currently married to Terri, his second wife. He has two minor children from his first marriage.

- Paul plans to leave $1 million to Terri and the remaining $4 million of business assets to his children.

The issues:

- The $1 million may not provide sufficient income for Terri.

- If Paul dies at an early age, his children may receive their inheritance before they are prepared for the responsibility.

- The estate taxes on the assets left to Paul's children are approximately $1.6 million, nearly half of their inheritance.

The solution:

- Leave $1 million directly to Terri.
  - Due to the unlimited marital deduction, no estate taxes are due.
- Leave the business in trust to his children.
- Establish a $2 million irrevocable life insurance trust for the children.
  - Proceeds are estate tax-free.
  - Trust provisions can establish distribution ages and requirements for the children.
- Establish a $2 million qualified terminable interest property (QTIP) trust for Terri.
  - Terri receives the interest income from the trust during her lifetime.

- She has the right to invade the principal of the trust under specified circumstances.
- Trust assets pass to Paul's children at Terri's death.

The result:

- Terri is provided with income throughout her lifetime.
- The children receive their assets in a controlled manner.
- The children still receive their full inheritance from their father.
- The estate taxes are provided for, eliminating the need to liquidate the business.

Example 6:
Survivor Income Needs

The situation:

- Ben, a business owner, has a total net worth of $3,550,000, consisting of:

Cash and securities	*$ 200,000*
Residence	*$ 450,000*
Building and land	*$ 650,000*
Business interest	*$1,750,000*
Corporate-owned life insurance	*$ 500,000*
Total assets:	***$3,550,000***

- At his death, Ben plans to leave the business (including the building, land, and life insurance) to his children, both of whom work in the business.

- The remaining assets will go to Diane, his wife.

The issues:

- Leaving the business to the children would create an immediate estate tax of almost $1 million—where would the money to pay this tax come from?

- As the surviving spouse, Diane would have only $200,000 of income-producing assets to live on. Assuming the money was generating an after-tax rate of 6%, her annual income would be only $12,000.

The solution:

- Place the insurance in an irrevocable trust, which removes it from the estate.

- Leave the building and land to the children in an exemption trust.

- Pass the remainder of the estate to Diane, including the corporate stock.

- Create a buy/sell agreement between Diane and the children and fund it with permanent life insurance.

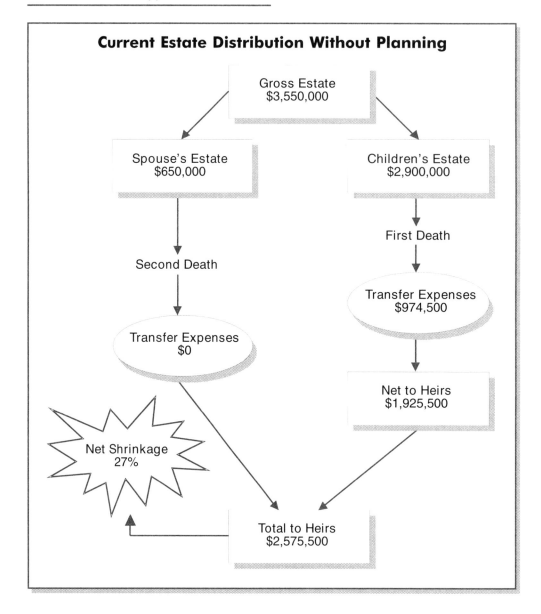

Current Estate Distribution Without Planning

Gross Estate
$3,550,000

Spouse's Estate
$650,000

Children's Estate
$2,900,000

First Death

Second Death

Transfer Expenses
$974,500

Transfer Expenses
$0

Net to Heirs
$1,925,500

Net Shrinkage
27%

Total to Heirs
$2,575,500

The result:

- With over $2 million of cash to invest, Diane should be able to generate an after-tax income of over $120,000 a year.

- Leaving the business to Diane with a buyout agreement eliminates the estate tax on the business at Ben's death.

- The children have been provided the money, income and estate tax-free, to buy the business from Diane.

- The business assets are removed from Diane's estate for estate tax purposes.

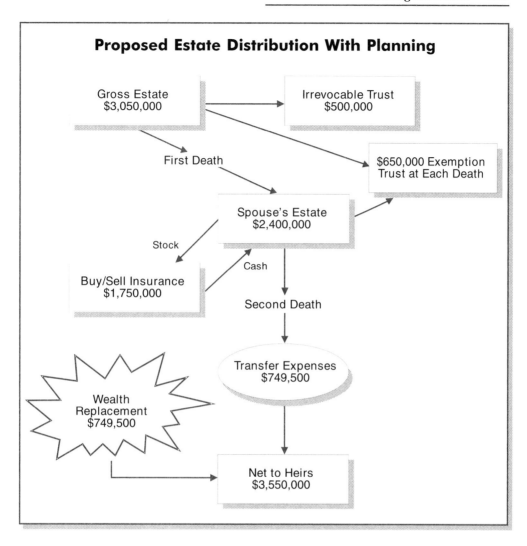

Proposed Estate Distribution With Planning

Gross Estate
$3,050,000

Irrevocable Trust
$500,000

First Death

$650,000 Exemption
Trust at Each Death

Spouse's Estate
$2,400,000

Stock

Cash

Buy/Sell Insurance
$1,750,000

Second Death

Transfer Expenses
$749,500

Wealth
Replacement
$749,500

Net to Heirs
$3,550,000

Example 7: Estate Liquidity Needs

The situation:

- Deborah, an unmarried business owner, has an estate of $5,650,000, consisting of:

Cash (including $200,000 IRA)	*$ 700,000*
Real estate	*$1,400,000*
Residence	*$ 900,000*
Vacation home	*$ 250,000*
Corporate stock	*$2,400,000*
Total assets:	***$5,650,000***

- Deborah's son works in the business. At her death, Deborah wants him to inherit the business, the real estate, and the vacation home ($4,050,000).

- She wants her daughter, who is not active in the business, to receive the cash and the home ($1,600,000).

The issues:

- The estate tax would be almost $2.4 million.

- After paying income taxes on the IRA, the cash is reduced to $620,000, leaving a liquidity shortfall of just under $1.8 million.

- Forced liquidation to pay the taxes could put the business at risk.

- Deborah's daughter could end up with nothing.

The solution:

- Deborah gifts the company stock to her son and the other assets to her daughter. She creates voting stock and non-voting stock, and uses her lifetime exemption with the stock gifted to her son. She gives the maximum in annual gifts each year and the balance at her death.

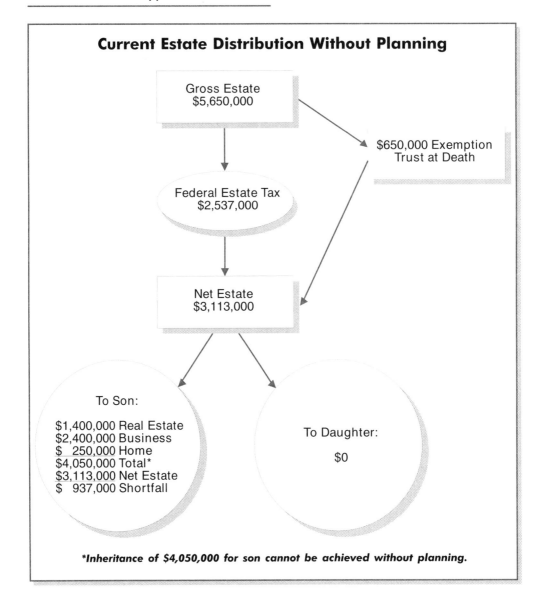

Current Estate Distribution Without Planning

Gross Estate
$5,650,000

$650,000 Exemption
Trust at Death

Federal Estate Tax
$2,537,000

Net Estate
$3,113,000

To Son:

$1,400,000 Real Estate
$2,400,000 Business
$ 250,000 Home
$4,050,000 Total*
$3,113,000 Net Estate
$ 937,000 Shortfall

To Daughter:

$0

Inheritance of $4,050,000 for son cannot be achieved without planning.

- She also creates an irrevocable life insurance trust in the amount of $2.4 million to fund the anticipated estate taxes.

The result:

- Deborah's son receives the business.
- Deborah's daughter receives the cash and the home.
- Life insurance provides the needed liquidity to pay estate taxes.
- The business doesn't have to be sold.

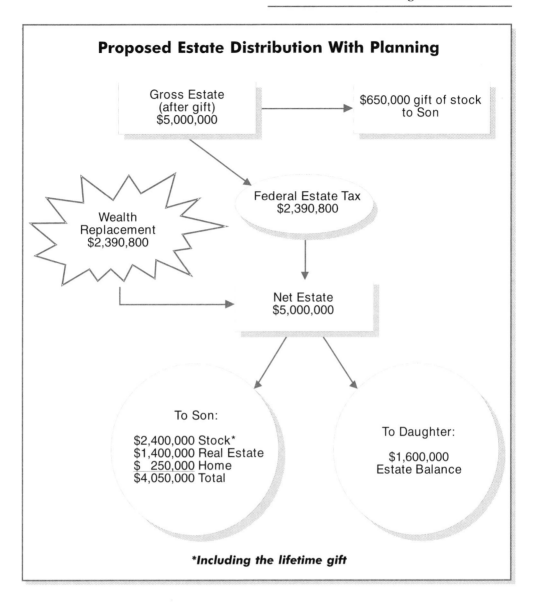

Proposed Estate Distribution With Planning

Gross Estate
(after gift)
$5,000,000

$650,000 gift of stock
to Son

Wealth
Replacement
$2,390,800

Federal Estate Tax
$2,390,800

Net Estate
$5,000,000

To Son:

$2,400,000 Stock*
$1,400,000 Real Estate
$ 250,000 Home
$4,050,000 Total

To Daughter:

$1,600,000
Estate Balance

Including the lifetime gift

Example 8:
Charitable Remainder Trust
and Wealth Replacement Trust

The situation:

- Lisa and Chris have $2 million of non-dividend paying stock that generates no income.

The issues:

- They want to generate $160,000 of income a year for themselves.
- They want to pass the $2 million to their children.
- They also want to donate $2 million to their favorite charity.

The solution:

- Create a wealth replacement trust, funded with a $2 million joint life second-to-die policy.
- Donate the stock to a charitable remainder trust, which sells the stock and reinvests the entire $2 million into an income-producing vehicle.

The result:

- The income from the charitable remainder trust generates the $160,000 a year Lisa and Chris wanted.
- At the second death, no estate taxes are due.
- The children receive their $2 million inheritance from the tax-free insurance proceeds.
- Their favorite charity receives $2 million (see the table on the next page).

Charitable Remainder Trust and Wealth Replacement Trust

	No Planning	With Charitable Bequest	With Bequest and WRT
Lifetime:			
Asset Value	$2,000,000	$2,000,000	$2,000,000
Annual Income	$0	$160,000*	$160,000*
Gift to WRT	n/a	n/a	($28,000)**
Net Annual Income	$0	$160,000	$132,000
At Death:			
Total Taxes:	$1,100,000	0	0
Insurance Proceeds:	n/a	n/a	$2,000,000
Net to Children	$900,000	0	$2,000,000
% to Children	45%	0	100%
Net to Charity	0	$2,000,000	$2,000,000
% to Charity	0	100%	100%
Total to Beneficiaries:	**$900,000**	**$2,000,000**	**$4,000,000**

 * Figure represents annual income from trust assuming 8% annual interest.
** Estimated annual cost for $2 million joint life second-to-die policy.

Appendix Three:

GLOSSARY

Administrator. A person or financial institution chosen by the probate court to represent and manage an estate when no will exists, or if no executor has been named.

Alternative Minimum Tax. A parallel tax system that recalculates tax without depreciation and other deductions that have no economic impact. It seeks to impose a tax based on real economic income without accounting preferences or other non-economic adjustments.

Annual Exclusion. See *Gift Tax Exclusion.*

Beneficiary. The person or organization receiving the benefits of a will, trust, life insurance policy, annuity, retirement plan, or similar device.

Benefit Cap. A limitation imposed on the computation of benefits. For example, employees receive disability coverage of 60% of salary up to $5,000 a month. This $5,000 a month is the benefit cap.

Bracket Shifting. The process of reordering financial affairs among family members to recognize income or estate taxes at the lowest possible rate. The brackets referred to are IRS tax brackets.

Buy/Sell Agreement. An agreement between partners or shareholders in a company to buy stock or partnership interest at a stated price upon the occurrence of certain events, such as death or disability.

Bypass Trust. A trust established at the death of the first spouse and funded with the federal estate tax applicable exclusion amount. The trust can make payments to the surviving spouse without subjecting its remaining assets to estate taxes at his or her death. All of the trust property passes estate tax-free to other beneficiaries at the death of the surviving spouse.

C Corporation. A corporation taxed under Subchapter C of the Internal Revenue Code. This type of corporation results in two levels of tax: at the corporate level and at a personal level.

Capital Gains Tax. A tax on the difference between the sales price and the adjusted basis of a capital asset.

Charitable Lead Trust. A charitable remainder trust in reverse. The charity receives payments for a term of years or for the donor's life. At the end of the period, the assets pass to a non-charitable beneficiary, typically the donor's child or grandchild. This is called a charitable lead trust because the charity's interest "leads" or comes before the private, non-charitable interest.

Charitable Remainder Trust. Appreciated assets, such as stock, are transferred to a charity in exchange for a payment (for example, 7%) for a term of years or for life. At the end of the term, the property is owned by the charity.

Closely Held Business. A privately owned business where the stock is not publicly traded.

Codicil. A written change or amendment to a will. To be valid, a codicil must be signed and witnessed in the same way as a will.

Community Property. In some states, property acquired during marriage by either spouse is considered to be automatically the property of both spouses. Each spouse generally has a right to dispose of half of this community property at death, regardless of whose name it is held in.

Credit For State Death Taxes. This credit reduces the federal estate tax. The credit is for state death taxes actually paid, but is limited to a maximum amount that varies with the size of the estate (the larger the estate, the higher the limit).

Credit Shelter Trust. See *Bypass Trust*.

Cross-Purchase Agreement. An agreement between shareholders to buy each other's stock at the occurrence of certain events, such as death or disability.

Crummey Power of Withdrawal. A method of changing a gift of future interest into a gift of present interest, which is eligible for the $10,000 annual exclusion. Refers to the right given in a trust to withdraw money, usually within a limited period of time, so that the money can be used immediately.

Death Tax. An estate tax or inheritance tax imposed on assets passing at death.

Deferred Compensation. Income for services earned presently but paid at a later date. Generally, there is a restriction that prevents current payment.

Dynasty Trust. A trust designed to benefit grandchildren and maximize use of the generation skipping exemption of $1 million GST gifting limit per donor. This trust can use life insurance to leverage the $1 million into several million.

Employee Stock Ownership Plan (ESOP). An IRS qualified plan where employees own stock in the corporation. The stock is owned by a trust, of which the employees are beneficiaries. Because the trust is considered a qualified plan, contributions to the ESOP can be made on a pre-tax basis.

Estate. The assets of a person, particularly a deceased person. The probate estate consists of assets owned in the person's sole name or payable to his or her estate (see *Probate*). When used in connection with the federal estate tax, however, "estate" refers to a broad range of assets over which the person had any rights or control. The federal estate is known as the "gross estate," and it includes all or part of such common assets as joint property, life insurance proceeds, and qualified retirement plans.

Estate Tax. A tax imposed on the value of all property interests held at death.

Executor. A person or organization named in a will to represent and manage an estate.

Exemption Equivalent. The amount of assets required to use the exemption from estate and gift taxes. The current $1,300,000 ($650,000 each for husband and wife) exemption saves $422,600 in estate taxes.

Family Attribution. Treating members of a family as one unit for certain purposes of the tax code.

Family Business. A business in which shareholders are all members of an extended family. Frequently, these businesses consist of members of several generations.

Family Limited Partnership (FLP). A device where one family member is a general partner and other family members are limited partners. The value of the limited partners' interest is frequently discounted due to lack of control and marketability. An FLP facilitates the transfer of assets to the next generation in a tax efficient manner.

Fiduciary Duty. The high degree of legal responsibility owed to beneficiaries by a trustee, executor, administrator, or guardian, each of whom is also referred to as a fiduciary.

Foundation. A charitable organization, either public or private, that distributes money for charitable purposes. It can be funded by a gift, such as appreciated stock. While it is subject to certain restrictions, income from its investments can be used to fund charitable programs.

Generation Skipping Transfer (GST) Tax. An additional tax imposed when a transfer is made from one generation directly to a third generation, skipping over the second generation (for example, from a grandparent to a grandchild).

Gift. A gratuitous transfer of property, either during life or at death. When made through a will, a gift of personal property is often called a "bequest" or "legacy," while a gift of real property is traditionally called a "devise" (see *Property*). For the purposes of the federal gift tax, a gift is a lifetime transfer of property for which full value is not received in return.

Gift Tax. A tax imposed on the value of property transferred during life. The federal gift tax is coordinated with the federal estate tax and uses the same tax rates and unified credit. A few states also have their own gift taxes. See *Estate Tax* and *Transfer Tax*.

Gift Tax Exclusion. The annual $10,000 per person exclusion from the federal or state gift tax laws. An individual may gift up to $10,000 to any number of people per year, free of gift taxes. The individuals do not have to be related. The annual exclusion is separate from, and in addition to, the unified credit.

Golden Handcuffs. A plan that pays benefits provided an individual adheres to his or her commitment to the company. These plans generally make payment of benefits contingent upon reaching certain goals. For example, if an employee remains in the employ of the company for 20 years, an annual retirement benefit of $50,000 will be paid.

Grantor. The person who creates a trust. Also called a "donor," "settler," or "trustor."

Grantor-Retained Annuity Trust (GRAT). A transfer of property is made in exchange for a payment from a trust. The transaction can be structured so that the transfer completely eliminates the property from the estate for tax purposes.

Guardian. A person or financial institution appointed by the probate court to oversee the affairs of a ward, who is either a minor or a legally incompetent person. A "guardian of the property" has authority over all assets of the ward, while a "guardian of the person" has authority over the ward's non-financial, personal life decisions.

Imputed Economic Benefit. The means of measuring the dollar value of the benefit of goods, property, or services provided by someone else.

Income With Respect to the Decedent. Income that is paid after the death of a person but is attributed to them for income tax purposes as if they received it before they died.

Incompetent. Lacking the mental capacity to act in one's own interest. A minor child lacks capacity by law as a result of his or her age. An adult, however, is legally incompetent only if found to be so by a court.

Inheritance Tax. The state death tax calculated on the amount received by a beneficiary.

Inter Vivos Trust. *See Living Trust.*

Intestacy. The condition of dying without leaving a valid will. A person who does so is said to be "intestate." In such cases, state law determines who inherits the probate property.

IRA (Individual Retirement Account). An account that is tax deferred until amounts are withdrawn after age 59½. Contributions may be made on either a pre-tax or post-tax basis, depending upon the person's income and qualified plan status at the time the contribution is made. The account may also act as a depository for amounts transferred from a pension or other retirement plan.

Irrevocable Trust. A trust whose governing provisions may not be revoked or amended after its creation. An irrevocable life insurance trust (ILIT) is a special type of irrevocable trust established for the purpose of protecting life insurance proceeds from estate taxes at the death of the insured person.

IRS Section 303. Advantageous tax treatment of distributions used to buy stock for the purpose of providing funds to pay estate taxes.

IRS Section 318. Constructive ownership of stock for certain purposes. Groups of family members are considered as one person for determining ownership for certain purposes of the IRS code, including the ownership percentage for determining whether dividend or capital gain tax will be paid upon the sale of a business.

IRS Section 6166. A statutory method of paying estate taxes that offers an installment payment plan at a lower interest rate for a certain portion of the taxes. The plan has various qualifications, and applies to only a portion of the estate.

Joint Property. Property held by two or more persons ("joint tenants"), each of whom owns a fractional share of the whole. The surviving owner or owners automatically receive the share of an owner who dies. It is often referred to as "joint tenancy" or "joint tenants with right of survivorship."

Keyperson. An important person to the corporation, someone who would be difficult to replace or cause economic damage if they were to leave. A life insurance policy is generally taken out on this person's life to protect the corporation in the event of their death.

Lifetime Exemption. An exemption from estate or gift tax given to every taxpayer. This allows the taxpayer to pass, during their lifetime by gift or at death, a specific amount free of transfer taxes. The amount is currently $650,000 per person and is scheduled to increase to $1 million by 2006. The benefit of this exemption is decreased by the higher marginal tax rates for estates over $10 million.

Limited Liability Company (LLC). When organized under the applicable state statue, a partnership that has the additional attribute of limited liability. This means that the shareholders have no personal liability beyond their own investment, and only one level of tax will be imposed.

Liquidation. The sale of a business, or stock in a business, to settle affairs.

Liquidity. The ability to turn assets into cash or cash equivalents. For example, cash is liquid, but stocks and bonds that have to be converted to cash and are less liquid. Real estate is considered illiquid because it is more difficult to convert to cash.

Living Trust. A trust that is established during the grantor's lifetime. This is often a revocable trust used to avoid probate and to distribute assets at the grantor's death. It is also known as an "inter vivos trust."

Marital Deduction. A gift tax or estate tax deduction for transfers of property between spouses. For federal gift tax and estate tax purposes this deduction is unlimited, meaning that property transferred to a spouse will not be taxed regardless of its value. This allows a married couple to postpone federal estate taxes until the death of the surviving spouse.

Non-Qualified Benefit Plan. A plan that does not qualify for favorable tax treatment under the IRS code because it is not required to be made available to all employees.

Personal Representative. An administrator or executor.

Phantom Stock Option Plan. A benefit plan based on the hypothetical value of stock. A value is set and then maintained. Under certain conditions, employees can receive the difference between the appreciated value of the phantom stock and its value when the plan was put into place.

Pour-Over Will. A will that leaves ("pours over") most or all of an estate to a trust (often a revocable living trust).

Power of Appointment. Transferring the right and responsibility to another person for the purpose of making decisions over the future ownership or disposition of assets. It is usually found in wills or trusts, but may be a separate document.

Power of Attorney. A document in which one person grants to another the legal right to perform specified activities on his of her behalf. It may be limited to certain activities (a "special" power of attorney) or may give broad power (a "general" power of attorney). Any power of attorney ends when the person who granted it dies. An "ordinary" power of attorney ends when the person who granted it becomes legally incompetent. A "durable" power of attorney, however, remains in effect even if the person granting it becomes legally incompetent.

Private Annuity. A stream of payments for a term of years, or for the lifetime of the annuitant, in exchange for a lump sum of money. This type of annuity is established between individuals or corporations, and is not an annuity or insurance product available to the general public.

Probate. The court-supervised process for managing and distributing the estate of a deceased person according to state laws or private instruments such as wills or trusts. Only probate property, consisting of assets held solely in the deceased person's name or payable to his or her estate, is subject to probate. Also refers to the process by which the government supervises the rights of children.

Property. In estate planning, the term is usually used in its broadest legal sense: anything over which legal rights of ownership may be held. It refers to all assets and is not limited to any one category (such as real estate). Real property refers to land and buildings; personal property refers to anything else.

Qualified Benefit Plans. Plans that qualify for favorable tax treatment under the IRS code, such as tax-free accumulation of income. Examples include pension plans, 401(k) plans, and Keogh plans. Generally, in exchange for the qualified status the plan is subject to certain restrictions (for example, coverage must be extended to all employees).

Qualified Personal Residence Trust (QPRT). A trust used to transfer personal residences in an estate tax advantaged manner. A residence is transferred to a trust in which the transferor retains the right to live in the home. This right is known as the "present interest." The ownership interest after the transferor's death, or the term of years of the trust, is known as the "remainder interest," which is transferred to the beneficiaries. Gift taxes are due only on the remainder interest.

Qualified Terminable Interest Property (QTIP) Trust. A type of trust under which the grantor gives his or her spouse all of the income from an asset, but no power to transfer the principal to anyone else. Assets placed in the trust qualify for the marital deduction under federal gift tax laws (if the trust is funded during the grantor's lifetime) or estate tax laws (if funded at death). Trust assets remaining at the surviving spouse's death are taxed as part of his or her estate.

Reverse Split-Dollar Plan. A split-dollar plan wherein the bulk of the death benefit in an employee-owned insurance policy is endorsed to the corporation for keyperson coverage purposes. The employer pays the economic benefit (PS-58) amount on the portion of the policy death benefit that is assigned to it. The balance of the premium is paid by the employee. When the endorsement is released, usually at retirement, the employee can access the entire cash value of the policy. The premium amount paid by the employee is frequently received in the form of a bonus, which may be grossed up for income tax purposes.

Revocable Trust. A trust that allows the grantor to revoke it, or to amend any of its terms. Funding the trust during life does not protect the grantor from income or estate taxes, but does remove these assets from probate.

Second-to-Die Life Insurance. An insurance policy covering two people that pays benefits at the death of the second person.

Self-Canceling Installment Note (SCIN). A note that cancels itself at the earlier of death of the lender or when the note is paid. This feature removes the note from the estate, but generally requires additional compensation so that the lending cost is higher than that of traditional lenders. Despite the higher cost, it is a valuable estate planning tool.

Sinking Fund. An account into which money is deposited and held for a specific future use, such as paying estate taxes or redeeming corporate stock.

Split-Dollar Life Insurance. A technique where the death benefit and cash value of an insurance policy are split and held by separate individuals or entities, typically an employer and employee. This generally helps individuals to acquire insurance on themselves that they would not be able to afford otherwise.

Step-Up in Basis. The increasing basis to fair market value at certain events, such as the death of the donor. This allows appreciated assets, such as stocks, to be passed on without paying capital gains taxes.

Stock Redemption Agreement. An agreement by which a shareholder sells his or her stock back to the corporation at a predetermined price at the occurrence of specified events such as death, disability, or separation of service. These agreements can be funded with life insurance.

Subchapter S Corporation. A corporation qualifying under Subchapter S of the IRS code. The corporation's earnings and expenses are passed through to the shareholder, resulting in one level of tax. Provides attributes similar to a partnership with the additional attribute of limited liability; however, it is subject to restrictions on the number of shareholders in the classes of stock.

Supplemental Disability Insurance. Disability insurance provided to an employee in addition to the available group coverage.

Supplemental Life Insurance. Life insurance provided to an employee in addition to the available group or other coverage.

Supplemental Retirement Plan. A non-qualified plan, often funded with insurance, which pays a benefit for a specified time after retirement. It may also contain a pre-retirement death benefit.

Tenancy in Common. A form of co-ownership whereby each owner (tenant) holds a fractional share of the property. Unlike "joint property" or a "tenancy by the entirety," each owner's share is probate property. At death, ownership passes through the owner's will (or by intestacy if there is no will), rather than passing automatically to the surviving joint owner(s).

Tenancy by the Entirety. A form of co-ownership that can exist only between spouses. Together, the spouses hold title to the whole property with right of survivorship. Upon the death of either spouse, the other automatically receives ownership of the whole. It can be terminated only by joint action of both spouses during their lives.

Testamentary Trust. A trust that is created in a will and takes effect only upon the testator's death.

Testate. The condition of dying and leaving a valid will.

Testator. One who has made a will.

Titling. The process of adjusting and formalizing the ownership of assets for efficient transfer at death.

Transfer Tax. The gift or estate tax levied on the transfer of assets from one person to another. See *Gift Tax* and *Estate Tax*.

Transfer for Value. Any transfer for a valuable consideration of the right to receive all or part of the proceeds of a life insurance policy. This causes the policy proceeds that exceed the premiums paid to be taxable as ordinary income under the transfer for value rule. Several exceptions exist, and in most situations, a transfer can be made that avoids the transfer for value rule.

Trust. A legal arrangement under which the grantor transfers ownership of assets to a trustee, who must manage and distribute the assets in the best interest of the trust's beneficiaries.

Trustee. The person or financial institution that holds legal title to property in trust for its beneficiaries. The trustee has a fiduciary duty to carry out the provisions of the trust in the best interest of the beneficiaries.

Unified Credit. A dollar amount, available to every taxpayer, which can be applied to reduce or eliminate federal estate and gift taxes. This amount can be transferred through any combination of lifetime and post-death gifts without any gift or estate taxes becoming due. See *Lifetime Exemption*.

Valuation. The process of determining the price paid by a willing buyer to a willing seller to purchase an asset. Many methods are available, including the income method, the net worth method, the cash flow method, and combinations thereof.

Wealth Replacement Trust (WRT). A trust used to provide insurance proceeds to replace the value of assets going to charity or to taxes.

Will. A legally binding document expressing a person's wishes on the distribution of his or her probate property, which takes effect at his or her death. To be valid, a will must conform to state law requirements.

Works Consulted

Adler, Robert J. "The Family Bank." *Journal of the American Society of CLU and ChFC*. Jan.1996: 44-49.

Aronoff, Craig E., and John L. Ward. *Family Business Succession: The Final Test of Greatness*. Marietta, GA: Business Owner Resources, 1992.

_____. *How to Choose and Use Advisors: Getting the Best Professional Family Business Advice*. Marietta, GA: Business Owner Resources, 1994.

Blackman, Irving. *Passing Your Business on to Your Family*. New York: Irwin, 1995.

Cohn, Mike. *Passing the Torch: Succession, Retirement, & Estate Planning in Family-Owned Businesses*. New York: McGraw-Hill, 1992.

Fowler, Thomas E. "How to Gain Credibility in the Business Market." 1997 MDRT Proceedings.

Giamarco, Julius H. "The Five Levels of Estate Planning." *LAN*. Oct. 1997.

Gibbs, Lawrence W. "Family Limited Partnership: All You Ever Wanted to Know." 1995 MDRT Proceedings.

Gunn, Eileen P. "How to Leave the Tax Man Nothing." *Fortune*. Mar. 18, 1996.

Kaye, Barry. *Save a Fortune on Your Estate Taxes*. Santa Monica, CA: Foreman, 1990.

Kettley, Richard M. "From Generation to Generation: Keeping the Family in the Business." 1995 MDRT Proceedings.

King, Al W. III. "From Dynasty to Remainderman: Utilizing the Dynasty Trust to Develop More Business." 1997 MDRT Proceedings.

Oshins, Richard A., and David R. Selznick. "Family Limited Partnerships and Limited Liability Companies: Comparisons and Planning Opportunities." 1996 MDRT Proceedings.

Shuntich, Louis S. *Estate and Business Planning After the Taxpayer Relief Act of 1997*. The American Society of CLU and ChFC, 1997.

Sun Life of Canada. *Building a Solid Estate Plan*. 1998.

Westhem, Andrew D. "Asset Protection through Advanced Estate Planning." 1997 MDRT Proceedings.

Index

A

B

C

D

I

K

L

M